Air Fryer Cookbook:

Over 100 Easy, Healthy & Low Carb Recipes for Beginners that Will Help Keep You Sane

Camilla Einersonn

Table of Contents

Introduction

Even if you are new to air frying, you will find that the recipes in this book are easy to follow and show the wide variety of meals, appetizers, and pastry dishes that you can easily make. You can even have the kids help! Most of the recipes cater to beginners and can be even made in less than half an hour. You will find an exciting array of recipes ranging from the staples in the American diet as well as an international chapter.

There are a few recipes that require more steps, but each recipe will provide you with an estimated preparation and cooking time, amount of servings, and a list of nutritional values including calories, net carbohydrates, protein, sugar, and fats. The recipes all include a simple-to-follow list of instructions to start feeding you and your family healthier meals today.

There are plenty of cookbooks featuring Air Frying in the market today, so thanks again for choosing this one! Every effort was made to ensure that it is full of as much useful information as possible. If you find the recipes in this cookbook enjoyable, please leave a review on Amazon.

Chapter 1: The Simplicity of Air Fryer Cooking

As you may know, the air fryer has become a sort of craze these last few years, and there are many reasons why. First off, it is extremely easy to use that even kids can run the machine. Therefore, even if you are not a master chef, you will be able to fry delicious and nutritious meals for you and your family.

Another reason why people love the air fryer so much is that it uses very little oil.

This helps to maintain the fried foods in your healthy diet since you will not be consuming the greasy fat that you normally would. In addition, it is quicker most of the time!

Many of the models come with a menu specific to what item you are cooking such as French fries, cakes, and fish. There also is the ease of pressing the settings you require and letting the air fryer work its magic while you do other tasks. It really cannot get much easier when everything is already figured out for you.

The cleanup is a breeze when it comes to air frying. Because there is no oil, you will not have to scrub pots and pans every night. There are also removable parts that you can easily stack in the dishwasher.

The beauty of the fryer is that you can insert oven-safe baking pans, ramekins, and silicone bakeware inside the basket with no issue. This results to less cleanup since you will be serving from the dish you are using to bake.

The time factor also helps make the air fryer very simple to use. You will find that most of your favorite dishes will now be served even more quickly and taste just as delicious.

This is especially the case with your fried foods, as you will still have the fantastic crunch factor that we all crave with deep-fried foods. Besides, since you are using little oil, you will be consuming much fewer calories while still enjoying your meal to the fullest.

If you find this cookbook So, are you ready to get started with these exciting recipes? Let us get to the good stuff: the recipes. Enjoy!

Chapter 2: Breakfast Recipes

Cinnamon Buns

Total Prep & Cooking Time: 20 minutes
Makes: 8 Buns
Protein: 2 gm.
Net Carbs: 23 gm.
Fat: 5 gm.
Sugar: 10 gm.
Calories: 150

What you need:

- 8 oz. container crescent rolls, refrigerated
- 1 tbsp. ground cinnamon
- 2 oz. raisins
- 1/3 cup butter
- 2 tbsp. sugar, granulated
- 1/3 cup pecans, chopped
- cooking spray (olive oil)
- maple syrup – 2 tbsp.
- 1/3 cup brown sugar

Steps:

1. In a saucepan, dissolve the butter completely. Transfer to a dish and blend the maple syrup and brown sugar.
2. Layer one 8-inch pan with the olive oil spray.
3. Distribute the sugar into the pan and empty the raisins and pecans inside, stirring to incorporate.
4. In a glass dish, whisk the sugar and ground cinnamon.
5. Open the can of crescent rolls and place on a cutting board.
6. Slice the entire log of dough into eight individual pieces.
7. Cover the top and bottom of the dough pieces in cinnamon and sugar, and transfer the pan to the air fryer.
8. Adjust the settings to air crisp at 345° F for 5 minutes.
9. Turn over the individual buns and steam for another 5 minutes.
10. Take the pan out and move the buns to a serving plate.

11. Drizzle the remaining sugar liquid on the buns and serve immediately.

Helpful Tip:

- You can customize your cinnamon buns with cream cheese, vanilla frosting, and dried cranberries or substitute the pecans for the walnuts if you prefer.

Egg and Cheese Veggie Cups

Total Prep & Cooking Time: 45 minutes
Makes: 4 Cups
Protein: 13 gm.
Net Carbs: 6 gm.
      Fat: 12 gm.
      Sugar: 0 gm.
      Calories: 195

What you need:

- cooking spray (olive oil)
- large eggs - 4
- 1/4 tsp. salt
- 2 oz. half & half
- cheddar cheese – 8oz, shredded
- 3 tsp. chopped cilantro
- 1/8 tsp. pepper

Steps:

1. Set the air fryer to the temperature of 300° F to heat.
2. Liberally spray 4 glass or ceramic ramekin dishes.
3. In a glass dish, blend the half & half, salt, cilantro, eggs, pepper and 4 oz. of the shredded cheese until combined.
4. Evenly distribute the mixture to the greased dishes.
5. Move the dishes to the basket in the air fryer for 12 minutes.
6. Once the time has passed, sprinkle the remaining 4 oz. of shredded cheese on top of each of the dishes.
7. Adjust the temperature to 400° F and broil for an additional 2 minutes.
8. Serve immediately and enjoy!

Helpful Tips:
- You can add in any of your favorites to these egg cups such as chopped vegetables or extra cheese, and customize them for different members of the family.
- Store any leftovers into a lidded tub and place in the fridge for approximately 4 days. When ready to eat, simply reheat them for half a minute in the microwave.

Egg in a Hole

Total Prep & Cooking Time: 5 minutes
Makes: 1 Helping
Protein: 9 gm.
Net Carbs: 21 gm.
Fat: 5 gm.
Sugar: 4 gm.
Calories: 170

What you need:

- Salt – ¼ tsp.
- 1 slice toast
- 1 large egg
- 1/8 tsp. pepper
- cooking spray (olive oil)

Steps:

1. Liberally spray the pan inside the air fryer with cooking spray.
2. Remove the middle of the slice of bread with a small cookie cutter and move to the pan.
3. Break the egg and put into the middle of the slice of bread.
4. Set the air fryer to heat at 330°F and cook for 6 minutes.
5. Use a metal spatula to turn the bread over and steam for an additional 4 minutes.
6. Serve hot and enjoy.

French Toast Sticks

Total Prep & Cooking Time: 15 minutes
Makes: 4 Helpings
Protein: 6 gm.
Net Carbs: 18 gm.
Fat: 8 gm.
Sugar: 7 gm.
Calories: 170

What you need:

- 1 tbsp. ground cinnamon
- 4 tbsp. butter
- 1 cup milk
- 5 large eggs
- 1/4 cup sugar, confectioner
- 12 slices Texas toast
- 1 tsp. vanilla extract

Steps:

1. In a hot saucepan, liquefy the butter completely.
2. Meanwhile, cut the bread into 3 separate pieces.
3. Using a glass dish, blend the vanilla extract, melted butter, milk, and eggs thoroughly.
4. In an additional glass dish, combine the sugar and ground cinnamon.
5. Dunk each slice of bread into the wet mixture and cover with the sugar mixture completely.
6. Transfer to a dish and blend the maple syrup and brown sugar.
7. Move to the air fryer basket and fry for approximately 8 minutes while setting at 350°F.
8. Remove the sticks from the air fryer and wait for approximately 5 minutes before serving.

Helpful Tip:
- Top your French Toast sticks with your favorite toppings of powdered sugar or maple syrup.

Ham and Cheese Omelet

Total Prep & Cooking Time: 15 minutes
Makes: 1 Omelet
Protein: 28 gm.
Net Carbs: 5 gm.
Fat: 18 gm.
Sugar: 1 gm.
Calories: 260

What you need:

- Salt - 1/4 tsp.
- Milk – 2 oz.
- cheddar cheese - 1/4 cup, shredded
- 6 tsp. ham, diced
- 1/3 tsp. thyme seasoning
- 2 tbsp. bell pepper, diced
- 6 tsp. mushrooms
- 2 large eggs
- 1/3 tsp. oregano seasoning
- 2 tbsp. onions, diced
- 1/3 tsp. paprika seasoning
- cooking spray (olive oil)

Steps:

1. Cover a 3x6-inch pan with olive oil spray.
2. Whisk the milk, salt, and eggs until blended in a glass dish.
3. Combine the diced ham, bell pepper, mushrooms, and, onions and stir until merged.
4. Transfer to the greased pan and move to the air fryer basket.
5. Adjust the temperature of the air fryer to 350°F and heat for approximately 5 minutes.
6. In a glass dish, combine the thyme, oregano, and paprika seasons.
7. Open the lid and sprinkle the seasonings evenly over the top. Then dust with the shredded cheese.
8. Steam for an additional 5 minutes. Use a rubber scraper to place between the omelet and the pan to lift up. Move to a serving plate and serve while hot.

Helpful Tip:
- You can substitute mozzarella cheese if you prefer in place of the cheddar cheese.

Hard-Boiled Eggs

Total Prep & Cooking Time: 20 minutes
Makes: 6 Eggs
Protein: 3 gm.
Net Carbs: 0 gm.
Fat: 0 gm.
Sugar: 0 gm.
Calories: 17

What you need:

- 6 large eggs, cold
- 4 cups of ice water

Steps:

1. Adjust the temperature of the air fryer to 250°F and insert the wire accessory into the basket.
2. Place the refrigerated eggs into the wire rack and heat for 16 minutes.
3. Remove the eggs to a dish of ice water.
4. Once cooled, peel the eggs and serve immediately.

Home Fries

Total Prep & Cooking Time: 30 minutes
Makes: 4 Helpings
Protein: 1 gm.
Net Carbs: 6 gm.
Fat: 1 gm.
Sugar: 0 gm.
Calories: 53

What you need:

- 1 tsp. salt
- 3 russet potatoes, cubed
- 1 tsp. chili powder
- 3 tbsp. of paprika seasoning
- olive oil - 2 tbsp.
- pepper - 1/2 tsp.
- garlic powder - 3 tbsp.

Steps:

1. Adjust the air fryer temperature to 400°F to heat.
2. Prepare the potatoes by scrubbing and chopping into cubes.
3. Using a glass dish, combine the cubed potatoes with paprika, olive oil, chili powder, and garlic powder until integrated.
4. In a single layer, assemble the potatoes in the air fryer basket. Fry for approximately 25 minutes.
5. Open the lid about every 10 minutes to toss the potatoes for it to be cooked fully.
6. Remove from the basket, distribute to a serving dish then serve immediately.

Loaded Hash Browns

Total Prep & Cooking Time: 55 minutes
Makes: 4 Helpings
Protein: 5 gm.
Net Carbs: 3 gm.
Fat: 8 gm.
Sugar: 1 gm.
Calories: 246

What you need:

- 2 garlic cloves, chopped
- 3 russet potatoes
- 2 oz. onions, chopped
- 1/4 cup red peppers, chopped
- 2 tsp. olive oil
- 1/4 tsp. salt
- 2 oz. cup green peppers, chopped
- 1 tsp. paprika seasoning
- 6 cups cold water
- 1/8 tsp. pepper

Steps:

1. Scrub the potatoes and remove the skins with a knife or vegetable peeler.
2. Use a cheese grater to shred the potatoes completely with the largest holes available. Transfer the potatoes to a glass dish.
3. Empty the cold water into the dish and saturate for approximately 20 minutes.
4. Empty the potatoes and remove the moisture thoroughly.
5. Set the temperature of the air fryer to heat at 400°F.
6. In an additional glass dish, blend the potatoes, olive oil, salt, garlic powder, paprika powder, and pepper until completely covered.
7. Transfer the potatoes to the air fryer basket and steam for 10 minutes.
8. Open the lid and combine the onion, garlic, and peppers to the basket. Toss ingredients to incorporate.

9. Heat for an additional 10 minutes and take out of the basket.
10. Wait for approximately 5 minutes before serving.

Maple-Glazed Bacon

Total Prep & Cooking Time: 20 minutes
Makes: 2 Omelets
Protein: 28 gm.
Net Carbs: 5 gm.
Fat: 18 gm.
Sugar: 1 gm.
Calories: 260

What you need:

- brown sugar - 3 tbsp.
- water - 2 tbsp.
- 8 slices bacon
- maple syrup - 2 tbsp.

Steps:

1. Adjust the air fryer to heat at 400°F. Remove the basket and cover the base with baking paper.
2. Empty the water into the base of the fryer while preheating.
3. In a glass dish, whisk the 2 tbsp. of maple syrup and the 3 tbsp. brown sugar together.
4. Place the wire rack into the basket and arrange the bacon into a single layer.
5. Spread the sugar glaze on the bacon until completely covered.
6. Put the basket into the air fryer and steam for 8 minutes.
7. Move the bacon from the basket and wait about 5 minutes before serving hot.

Helpful Tip:
- If the sugar glaze is too thick, simply add a small amount of maple syrup until the desired consistency.

Sausage, Egg, and Cheese Biscuits

Total Prep & Cooking Time: 45 minutes
Makes: 5 Biscuits
Protein: 7 gm.
Net Carbs: 13 gm.
Fat: 13 gm.
Sugar: 3 gm.
Calories: 190

What you need:

- pepper - 1/8 tsp.
- 10.2 oz. can biscuits, flaky
- 1/8 tsp. salt
- 1 1/2 tsp. vegetable oil
- 2oz. sharp cheddar cheese, cubed in 10 pieces
- 1 1/2 large eggs
- 1/8 lb. sausage, ground
- 1 1/2 tsp. water
- cooking spray (olive oil)

Steps:

1. Create an 8-inch circle of baking lining and set on the base of the basket of the air fryer. Cover with cooking spray. Set a separate piece of baking lining to the side.
2. Using a hot skillet, empty the oil and brown the sausage for approximately 4 minutes while breaking into small pieces with a wooden spatula.
3. Whip 2 of the eggs in a dish and blend with pepper and salt.
4. Remove the browned meat with a slotted ladle to a separate glass dish.
5. Adjust the temperature to medium. Empty the egg mixture and heat for about 60 seconds then combine with the cooked sausage dish and mix completely.
6. In the meantime, section the biscuit pastry into 5 pieces and transfer to the sheet of the baking lining.
7. Compress each into a thin circle and spoon a generous tablespoon of the meat and eggs into the middle.
8. Set a cube of cheese on the filling and enclose completely by

pinching the sides of the pastry.
9. In a glass dish, combine the water and remaining egg until smooth.
10. Apply the egg wash to each of the biscuits, covering entirely.
11. Transfer to the basket with the pinched sides on the baking lining.
12. Adjust the temperature to 325°F and heat for 10 minutes.
13. Carefully flip the biscuits carefully and continue steaming for 6 minutes more.
14. Remove the biscuits to a plate and enjoy!

Sausage Patties

Total Prep & Cooking Time: 45 minutes
Makes: 6 Patties
Protein: 9 gm.
Net Carbs: 1 gm.
Fat: 17 gm.
Sugar: 0 gm.
Calories: 190

What you need:
- onion powder - 1/2 tsp.
- 11 oz. of sausage, ground and cold
- red chili flakes - 1/2 tsp.
- thyme seasoning - 1/4 tsp.
- salt - 1/8 tsp.
- paprika seasoning - 1/4 tsp.
- garlic - 1 1/2 tsp., minced
- brown sugar - 1 tsp.
- cayenne pepper - 1/4 tsp.
- Tabasco sauce - 1 tsp.
- Pepper - 1/8 tsp.

Steps:

1. Cover a baking tray with baking lining and place into the air fryer basket.
2. Mix by hand the cold ground sausage with all the listed seasonings, Tabasco sauce, and brown sugar.
3. Divide the meat into 6 sections and create individual patties.
4. Move the patties to the basket in a single layer and adjust the air fryer to heat at 370° F.
5. Heat for 10 minutes and turn the patties to the other side.
6. Continue to broil for 10 additional minutes.
7. Remove from basket to a serving platter and enjoy.

Helpful Tips:
- Top the patties with additional tobacco sauce if you prefer a spicier patty.
- Alternatively, you can substitute lean pork or chicken sausage in this recipe.
- If you do not have brown sugar on hand, you can substitute maple syrup.

Savory Bagel Bites

Total Prep & Cooking Time: 30 minutes
Makes: 6 Bites
Protein: 5 gm.
Net Carbs: 23 gm.
Fat: 0 gm.
Sugar: 1 gm.
Calories: 130

What you need:

- 1 cup self-rising flour
- 8 oz. Greek yogurt
- 1/2 cup cream cheese, whipped
- cooking spray (olive oil)

Steps:

1. In a food blender, whip the yogurt and flour until it thickens into a dough for about 2 minutes.
2. Cover the base of the pan with cooking spray.
3. Create equal sized balls of the dough and move to the greased pan.
4. Shut the air fryer top and adjust the temperature to 325°F for about 5 minutes.
5. Turn the balls over and reset at the same temperature on the air crisp setting for 4 minutes.
6. Remove the balls from the basket and let it cool for approximately 10 minutes.
7. Poke a little hole into the sides of the bagels.
8. Pack the whipped cream cheese inside the holes using a pastry bag and serve immediately.

Helpful Tip:
- You can easily create a homemade pastry bag with a large-sized ziplock bag. Add the cream cheese and slice the bottom corner with scissors.
- If you would like a sweeter version, apply 1/2 teaspoon each of ground cinnamon and sugar to the balls after step 3. If you would like them even sweeter, apply another 1/2 teaspoon each of sugar and ground cinnamon and sugar during step 12.

Stuffed Baked Avocado

Total Prep & Cooking Time: 20 minutes
Makes: 2 Helpings
Protein: 11 gm.
Net Carbs: 3 gm.
Fat: 6 gm.
Sugar: 0 gm.
Calories: 281

What you need:

- Two eggs, preferably large
- Salt - 1/4 tsp.
- 1 avocado, large
- parsley seasoning - 3 tsp.
- cheddar - 2 oz., shredded
- Pepper - 1/8 tsp.

Steps:

1. Set the air fryer to the temperature of 400°F.
2. Pit the avocado by slicing in half and break the eggs into the hollow of the avocado.
3. Sprinkle the pepper, parsley, and salt on top of the whole of the avocados.
4. Move the avocado halves into the basket and heat for approximately 14 minutes.
5. Remove to a serving plate and dust with the shredded cheese before serving.

Sweet Potato Toast

Total Prep & Cooking Time: 40 minutes
Makes: 4 Helpings
Protein: 28 gm.
Net Carbs: 4.9 gm.
Fat: 18 gm.
Sugar: 1 gm.
Calories: 260

What you need:

- Salt - 1/4 tsp.
- paprika seasoning - 1/8 tsp.
- avocado oil - 4 tsp.
- garlic powder - 1/8 tsp.
- 1 sweet potato
- onion powder - 1/8 tsp.
- pepper - 1/4 tsp.
- oregano seasoning - 1/8 tsp.

Steps:

1. Heat the air fryer to the temperature of 380°F.
2. Cut the ends off the sweet potato and discard. Divide into 4 even pieces lengthwise.
3. Whisk the avocado oil and all of the seasonings until combined thoroughly.
4. Brush the spices on top of the slices of sweet potato.
5. Transfer the slices to the air fryer basket and fry for 15 minutes.
6. Turn the sweet potato pieces over and steam once again for 15 more minutes.
7. Remove to a serving plate and enhance with your preferred toppings.

Tomato Mushroom Frittata

Total Prep & Cooking Time: 30 minutes
Makes: 2 Helpings
Protein: 14 gm.
Net Carbs: 4 gm.
Fat: 14 gm.
Sugar: 2 gm.
Calories: 75

What you need:

- skim milk - 2 tbsp.
- pepper - 1/8 tsp.
- chives - 2 tbsp., chopped
- tomato - 1/4 cup, sliced
- egg whites - 8 oz.
- mushrooms - 1/4 cup, sliced

Steps:

1. Adjust the temperature of the air fryer to 320°F.
2. Using a glass dish, blend the tomato, egg whites, mushrooms and milk until combined.
3. Incorporate the seasonings of chives and pepper into the mixture.
4. Empty into the skillet and warm for about 15 minutes.
5. Serve immediately and enjoy while hot.

Chapter 3: Lunch Recipes

Bacon Cheddar Chicken Fingers

Total Prep & Cooking Time: 20 minutes
Makes: 4 Helpings
Protein: 24 gm.
Net Carbs: 6 gm.
Fat: 26 gm.
Sugar: 1 gm.
Calories: 192

What you need:

For the chicken fingers:
- 1 lb. chicken tenders, about 8 pieces
- cooking spray (canola oil)
- cheddar cheese - 1 cup, shredded
- Two eggs, large
- 1/3 cup bacon bits
- 2 tbsp. water

For the breading:
- 1 tsp. of onion powder
- panko bread crumbs - 2 cups
- black pepper - 1 tsp., freshly ground
- paprika - 2 tbsp.
- garlic powder - 1 tsp.
- salt - 2 tsp.

Steps:

1. Set the air fryer to the temperature of 360°F.
2. In a glass dish, whip the water and eggs until combined.
3. Use a zip lock bag, shake the garlic powder, salt, breadcrumbs, cayenne, onion powder, and pepper together.
4. Immerse the chicken into the eggs and shake in the ziplock bag until fully covered.
5. Dip again in the egg mixture and back into the seasonings until a thick coating is present.
6. Remove the tenders from the bag and set in the frying pan

29

in the basket. Do them in batches if need to not over pack the pan.

7. Apply the canola oil spray to the top of the tenders and heat for 6 minutes.
8. Flip the tenders to the other side. Steam for another 4 minutes.
9. Blend the bacon bits and shredded cheese in a dish.
10. Evenly dust the bacon and cheese onto the hot tenders and fry for 2 more minutes.
11. Remove and serve while hot.

Battered Cod

Total Prep & Cooking Time: 30 minutes
Makes: 4 Helpings
Protein: 35 gm.
Net Carbs: 3 gm.
Fat: 10 gm.
Sugar: 0 gm.
Calories: 371

What you need:

- Cod - 20 oz.
- Salt - 1/4 tsp.
- all-purpose flour - 8 oz.
- parsley seasoning - 1 tbsp.
- cornstarch - 3 tsp.
- garlic powder - 1/2 tsp.
- Two eggs, preferably large
- onion powder - 1/2 tsp.

Steps:

1. Whip the eggs in a glass dish until smooth and set to the side.
2. In a separate dish, blend the cornstarch, salt, almond flour, garlic powder, parsley, and onion powder, whisking to remove any lumpiness.
3. Immerse the pieces of cods into the egg and then into the spiced flour, covering completely.
4. Transfer to the fryer basket in a single layer.
5. Heat the fish for 7 minutes at a temperature of 350°F. Turn the cod over and steam for an additional 7 minutes.

Helpful Tip:
- Combine this fish dish with the *French fries* recipe, and you will have a Fish & Chips meal.

Beef Kabobs

Total Prep & Cooking Time: 30 minutes in addition to 1 hour
marinating time
Makes: 4 Kabobs
Protein: 23 gm.
Net Carbs: 4 gm.
Fat: 15 gm.
Sugar: 2 gm.
Calories: 250

What you need:

- low-fat sour cream - 1/3 cup
- one bell pepper
- 16 oz. of beef chuck ribs, boneless
- soy sauce - 2 tbsp.
- 6-inch skewers - 8
- Pepper - 1/4 tsp.
- medium onion - 1/2

Steps:

1. Slice the ribs into sections about 1-inch wide
2. In a lidded tub, combine the soy sauce, ribs and sour cream
   making sure the meat is fully covered.
3. Refrigerate for half an hour at least, if not overnight.
4. Immerse the wooden skewers for approximately 10 minutes
   in water.
5. Set the temperature of the air fryer to 400°F.
6. Slice the onion and bell pepper in 1-inch sections.
7. Remove the meat from the marinade, draining well.
8. Layer the onions, beef and bell peppers on the skewers and
   dust with pepper.
9. Heat for 10 minutes, ensuring you spin the skewers 5
   minutes into cooking time.
10. Serve while hot and enjoy.

Helpful Tips:
- There are other cuts of meat that will work for this recipe
  including sirloin steak and stew beef.

Cheese Dogs

Total Prep & Cooking Time: 15 minutes
Makes: 4 Hot Dogs
Protein: 12 gm.
Net Carbs: 29 gm.
Fat: 13 gm.
Sugar: 2 gm.
Calories: 288

What you need:

- 4 hotdogs
- 1/4 cup your choice of cheese, grated
- 4 hotdog buns

Steps:

1. Adjust the air fryer to heat at a temperature of 390°F for approximately 5 minutes.
2. Set the hot dogs in the basket and broil for 5 minutes.
3. Remove and create the hot dog with the bun and cheese as desired and move back to the basket for another 2 minutes.
4. Remove and enjoy while hot.

Cheeseburger Patties

Total Prep & Cooking Time: 20 minutes
Makes: 4 Patties
Protein: 35 gm.
Net Carbs: 0 gm.
Fat: 30 gm.
Sugar: 0 gm.
Calories: 425

What you need:

- garlic - 1/2 clove, minced
- ground beef - 1 1/3 cup
- onion - 4 oz., diced
- Worcestershire sauce - 2 tbsp.
- one egg, large
- panko breadcrumbs - 2 oz.
- cayenne pepper - 1/8 tsp.
- cooking spray (olive oil)
- salt - 1/4 tsp.
- 4 slices of cheese of your choice
- 1/8 tsp. pepper

Steps:

1. Using a big glass dish, combine the diced onion, pepper, minced garlic, cayenne pepper, breadcrumbs, and salt until incorporated.
2. Blend the ground beef, Worcestershire sauce, and egg and integrate thoroughly by hand.
3. Form the meat into 4 individual patties and move to the air fryer basket.
4. Coat the patties with cooking spray.
5. Adjust the temperature for 375°F and heat for 8 minutes.
6. Turn the burgers over and steam for an additional 2 minutes.
7. Cover with a slice of cheese and continue cooking for approximately 3 minutes.
8. Enjoy as is or place on a bun with your favorite toppings.

Helpful Tips:
- This is for a medium well burger. If you prefer a rare or medium burger, heat for a total of 10 minutes. For well done, it will be a total of 15 minutes to cook.

Chicken Cordon Bleu

Total Prep & Cooking Time: 35 minutes
Makes: 4 Helpings
Protein: 24 gm.
Net Carbs: 6 gm.
Fat: 26 gm.
Sugar: 1 gm.
Calories: 192

What you need:

- Pepper - 1/4 tsp.
- chicken paillards - 4
- salt - 1/4 tsp.
- Swiss cheese - 8 slices
- all-purpose flour - 1/2 cup
- parmesan cheese - 2/3 cup, grated
- panko breadcrumbs - 1 1/2 cup
- ham - 8 slices
- two eggs, large
- Dijon mustard - 2 tbsp.
- 8 toothpicks
- grapeseed oil spray

Steps:

1. On a section of baking lining, brush the Dijon mustard on each chicken paillard and sprinkle with pepper and salt
2. Layer 1 cheese, 2 slices of the ham and then the additional slice of cheese on each of the pieces of chicken.
3. Rotate the chicken beginning with the longer side to create a roll. Fasten in place with two toothpicks.
4. Whip the egg in one dish, empty the flour into a second dish and blend the parmesan cheese and breadcrumbs into a third.
5. Immerse one chicken first in flour, secondly immerse in the egg and then roll the chicken completely in the breadcrumbs. Press the cheese and breadcrumbs into the chicken to secure and place onto a plate.
6. Repeat for the other pieces of chicken.

7. Apply the grapeseed oil spray to each section of chicken and transfer to the air fryer basket after 5 minutes.
8. Set the air fryer temperature to heat at 350°.
9. Grill for 8 minutes and carefully turn the chicken to the other side. Heat for an additional 8 minutes.
10. Remove to a serving dish and wait approximately 5 minutes before serving hot.

Helpful Tip:
- You can alternatively use Italian flavored panko breadcrumbs to add more flavor to the recipe.

Grilled Cheese Sandwich

Total Prep & Cooking Time: 10 minutes
Makes: 1 Sandwich
Protein: 17 gm.
Net Carbs: 22 gm.
Fat: 8 gm.
Sugar: 2 gm.
Calories: 220

What you need:

- 2 slices bread, softened
- 1 tsp. butter
- 2 slices cheddar cheese

Steps:

1. Set the air fryer at a temperature of 350°F.
2. Apply 1/2 teaspoon of the softened butter to one side of the slice of bread. Repeat for the remaining bread.
3. Create the sandwich by putting the cheese in between the non-buttered sides of bread.
4. Transfer to the hot air fryer and set for 5 minutes. Flip the sandwich at the halfway point and remove.
5. Serve immediately and enjoy.

Helpful Tip:
- Alternatively, add 2 slices of turkey or ham to this sandwich and cook for an additional 2 minutes.

Italian Meatballs

Total Prep & Cooking Time: 35 minutes
Makes: 3 Helpings
Protein: 24 gm.
Net Carbs: 6 gm.
Fat: 26 gm.
Sugar: 1 gm.
Calories: 192

What you need:

- one egg, large
- ground beef - 16 oz.
- pepper - 1/8 tsp.
- oregano seasoning - 1/2 tsp.
- bread crumbs - 1 1/4 cup
- garlic - 1/2 clove, chopped
- parsley - 1 oz., chopped
- salt - 1/4 tsp.
- Parmigiano-Reggiano cheese - 1 oz. cup, grated
- cooking spray (avocado oil)

Steps:

1. Whisk the oregano, breadcrumbs, chopped garlic, salt, chopped parsley, pepper, and grated Parmigiano-Reggiano cheese until combined.
2. Blend the ground beef and egg into the mixture using your hands. Incorporate the ingredients thoroughly.
3. Divide the meat into 12 sections and roll into rounds.
4. Coat the inside of the basket with avocado oil spray to grease.
5. Adjust the temperature to 350°F and heat for approximately 12 minutes.
6. Roll the meatballs over and steam for another 4 minutes and remove to a serving plate.
7. Enjoy as is or combine with your favorite pasta or sauce.

Helpful Tip:
- If you want to help with cleanup, simply cut a piece of baking lining to fit the base of your air frying pan.
- Are you out of breadcrumbs? You can use a few slices of going stale bread and crumble in a food blender.

Loaded Baked Potatoes

Total Prep & Cooking Time: 25 minutes
Makes: 4 Helpings
Protein: 24 gm.
Net Carbs: 6 gm.
Fat: 26 gm.
Sugar: 1 gm.
Calories: 192

What you need:

- 1/3 cup milk
- 2 oz. sour cream
- 1/3 cup white cheddar, grated
- 2 oz. Parmesan cheese, grated
- 1/8 tsp. garlic salt
- 6 oz. ham, diced
- 2 medium russet potatoes
- 4 oz. sharp cheddar, shredded
- 1/8 cup. green onion, diced

Steps:

1. Puncture the potatoes deeply with a fork a few time and microwave for approximately 5 minutes. Flip them to the other side and nuke for an additional 5 minutes. The potatoes should be soft.
2. Use oven mitts to remove from the microwave and cut them in halves.
3. Spoon out the insides of the potatoes to about a quarter-inch from the skins and distribute the potato flesh to a glass bowl.
4. Combine the parmesan, garlic salt, sour cream, and white cheddar cheese to the potato dish and incorporate fully.
5. Distribute the mixture back to the emptied potato skins. Create a small hollow in the middle by pressing with a spoon.
6. Divide the ham evenly between the potatoes and place the ham inside the hollow.
7. Position the potatoes in the fryer and set the air fryer to the

temperature of 300°F.

8. Heat for 8 minutes and then sprinkle the cheddar cheese on top of each potato.
9. Melt the cheese for two more minutes then serve with diced onions on top.

Helpful Tip:
- You can make these up to 5 days ahead and refrigerate until you are prepared to fry. Simply cover with plastic wrap or store in a lidded tub.

Pepperoni Pizza

Total Prep & Cooking Time: 10 minutes
Makes: 1 Pizza
Protein: 6 gm.
Net Carbs: 28 gm.
Fat: 6 gm.
Sugar: 1 gm.
Calories: 200

What you need:

- 1 mini naan flatbread
- 2 tbsp. pizza sauce
- 7 slices mini pepperoni
- 1 tbsp. olive oil
- 2 tbsp. mozzarella cheese, shredded

Steps:

1. Prepare the naan flatbread by brushed the olive oil on the top.
2. Layer the naan with pizza sauce, mozzarella cheese, and pepperoni.
3. Transfer to the frying basket and set the air fryer to the temperature of 375°F.
4. Heat for approximately 6 minutes and enjoy immediately.

Helpful Tips:
- You can put any of your favorite toppings on this pizza. Keep an eye as to when the cheese melts and allow to air fry for an additional 2 minutes.

Southern Style Fried Chicken

Total Prep
& Cooking Time: 25   minutes
Makes: 6 Helpings
Protein: 24 gm.
Net Carbs: 6 gm.
Fat: 26 gm.
Sugar: 1 gm.
Calories: 192

What you need:

- Italian seasoning - 1 tsp.
- chicken legs or breasts - 2 lbs.
- Buttermilk - 2 tbsp.
- paprika seasoning - 1 1/2tsp.
- cornstarch - 2 oz.
- onion powder - 1 tsp.
- hot sauce - 3 tsp.
- pepper - 1 1/2 tsp.
- 2 large eggs
- 1 cup self-rising flour
- 2 tsp. salt
- cooking spray (olive oil)
- 1/4 cup water
- garlic powder - 1 1/2tsp.

Steps:

1. Clean the chicken by washing thoroughly and pat dry with paper towels.
2. Use a glass dish to blend the pepper, paprika, garlic powder, onion powder, salt, and Italian seasoning.
3. Rub approximately 1 tablespoon of the spices into the pieces of chicken to cover entirely.
4. Blend the cornstarch, flour, and spices by shaking in a large ziplock bag.
5. In a separate dish, combine the eggs, hot sauce, water, and milk until integrated.

6. Completely cover the spiced chicken in the flour and then immerse in the eggs.

7. Coat in the flour for a second time and set on a tray for approximately 15 minutes.

8. Before transferring the chicken to the air fryer, spray liberally with olive oil and space the pieces out, frying a separate batch if required.

9. Adjust the temperature to 350° F for approximately 18 minutes.

10. Take the chicken out and set on a plate. Wait about 5 minutes before serving.

Baking Tip:
- To ensure a crispy breading on the chicken, make sure that you do not overcoat with the egg or flour mixture.

Stuffed Bell Peppers

Total Prep & Cooking Time: 30 minutes
Makes: 2 Peppers
Protein: 25 gm.
Net Carbs: 22 gm.
Fat: 5 gm.
Sugar: 1 gm.
Calories: 210

What you need:

- medium onion - 1/2, chopped
- cheddar cheese - 4 oz., shredded
- pepper - 1/2 tsp.
- ground beef - 8 oz.
- olive oil - 1 tsp.
- tomato sauce - 4 oz.
- Worcestershire sauce - 1 tsp.
- medium green peppers - 2, stems and seeds discarded
- salt - 1 tsp., separated
- water - 4 cups
- garlic - 1 clove, minced

Steps:

1. Boil the water in pot steam the green peppers with the tops and seeds removed with 1/2 teaspoon of the salt. Move from the burner after approximately 3 minutes and drain.
2. Pat the peppers with paper towels to properly dry.
3. In a hot frying pan, melt the olive oil and toss the garlic and onion for approximately 2 minutes until browned. Drain thoroughly.
4. Set the air fryer temperature to 400°F to warm up.
5. Using a glass dish, blend the beef along with Worcestershire sauce, 2 ounces of tomato sauce, salt, vegetables, 2 ounces of cheddar cheese and pepper until fully incorporated.
6. Spoon the mixture evenly into the peppers and drizzle the remaining 2 ounces of tomato sauce on top. Then dust with the remaining 2 ounces of cheddar cheese.
7. Assemble the peppers in the basket of the air fryer and heat

fully for approximately 18 minutes. The meat should be fully cooked before removing.

8. Place on a platter and serve immediately.

Tuna Patties

Total Prep & Cooking Time: 20 minutes
Makes: 4 Helpings
Protein: 6 gm.
Net Carbs: 4 gm.
Fat: 2 gm.
Sugar: 0 gm.
Calories: 58

What you need:

- garlic powder - 1 tsp.
- tuna - 2 cans, in water
- dill seasoning - 1 tsp.
- all-purpose flour - 4 tsp.
- salt - 1/4 tsp.
- mayonnaise - 4 tsp.
- lemon juice - 2 tbsp.
- onion powder - 1/2 tsp.
- pepper - 1/4 tsp.

Steps:

1. Set the temperature of the air fryer to 400°F.
2. Combine the almond flour, mayonnaise, salt, onion powder, dill, garlic powder and pepper using a food blender for approximately 30 seconds until incorporated.
3. Empty the canned tuna and lemon juice into the blender and pulse for an additional 30 seconds until integrated fully.
4. Divide evenly into 4 sections and create patties by hand.
5. Transfer to the fryer basket in a single layer and heat for approximately 12 minutes.

Helpful Tips:
- If you should have canned tuna packed in oil, it will work if you add an additional 2 teaspoons of almond flour to the mixture. This is also the case if the meat is too wet.

Chapter 4: Bread and Roll Recipes

Banana Bread

Total Prep & Cooking Time: 50 minutes
Makes: 4 Helpings
Protein: 3 gm.
Net Carbs: 22 gm.
Fat: 6 grams
Sugar: 14 grams
Calories: 155

What you need:

- all-purpose flour - 2 cups
- canola oil - 1/2 cup
- baking powder - 2 tsp.
- four medium bananas, peeled
- sugar - 2/3 cup, granulated
- sour cream - 1/3 cup
- two large eggs
- peanut butter - 4 tbsp., creamy
- salt - 1/2 tsp.
- cooking spray (olive oil)
- walnuts - 1 1/2 cup, roughly chopped
- vanilla extract - 2 tsp.
- baking soda - 1/2 tsp.

Steps:

1. Adjust the air fryer temperature to 330°F. Coat the sides and base of a pan with olive oil spray.
2. Use a food blender, pulse the bananas for about 30 seconds until creamy.
3. Combine the sour cream, baking soda, eggs, peanut butter, salt, sugar, vanilla extract, and oil until thoroughly integrated for about 90 seconds.
4. Blend the flour and baking powder into the dough and pulse for an additional 30 seconds.
5. Using a rubber scraper, blend the walnuts until fully

incorporated.
6. Empty into the prepped pan and smooth with the rubber scraper until even throughout.
7. Transfer the pan to the air fryer basket and heat for approximately 35 minutes.
8. Remove from the air fryer to a wire rack. Wait about 10 minutes before flipping onto a cutting board.
9. Slice into 4 equal pieces and serve warm.

Helpful Tips:
- Substitute Greek yogurt for the sour cream if you wish to have more moist bread.
- If you would rather have sweeter banana bread, you can alternatively use 3/4 cup of chocolate chips in place of the walnuts.
- The bread can be stored for 7 days in a lidded tub on the counter or for 3 months in the freezer.

Chocolate Croissants

Total Prep & Cooking Time: 10 minutes
Makes: 8 Croissants
Protein: 2 gm.
Net Carbs: 14 gm.
Fat: 6 gm.
Sugar: 6 gm.
Calories: 110

What you need:

- 8 oz. can croissant rolls
- 1/2 cup chocolate chips

Steps:

1. Open the can of croissant rolls and completely unroll the individual slices of dough onto a piece of baking lining.
2. Arrange a line of approximately 6 chocolate chips on the longer end of the dough and rotate into a roll.
3. Move the croissants to the basket of the air fryer and heat to the temperature of 320°F for about 4 minutes.
4. Flip the rolls over and fry for another 2 minutes.
5. Serve immediately and enjoy!

Corn Bread

Total Prep & Cooking Time: 35 minutes
Makes: 4 Helpings
Protein: 4 gm.
Net Carbs: 27 gm.
Fat: 5 gm.
Sugar: 2 gm.
Calories: 174

What you need:

- Cornmeal - 1 cup
- Sugar - 3 tsp., granulated
- Butter - 6 tbsp., unsalted and melted
- baking powder - 1 1/2 tsp.
- all-purpose flour - 3/4 cup
- baking soda - 1/2 tsp.
- Two eggs, large
- Salt - 1/4 tsp.
- butter - 2 tbsp., unsalted
- buttermilk - 12 oz.

Steps:

1. Dissolve the 2 tablespoons of butter in a saucepan. Rub on the inside and base of an 8-inch pan. Set the baking pan to the side.
2. Adjust the temperature on the air fryer to heat at 360°F.
3. In a glass dish, whisk the baking powder, sugar, salt, baking soda, flour, and cornmeal until there are no lumps present.
4. Blend the 6 tablespoons of butter, eggs, and buttermilk into the dish and completely integrate. The consistency will be slightly lumpy.
5. Distribute the batter to the prepped pan and place inside the air fryer basket.
6. Fry for a total of 25 minutes and remove. Slice after approximately 10 minutes and enjoy!

Garlic Cheese Buns

Total Prep & Cooking Time: 10 minutes
Makes: 4 Rolls
Protein: 2 gm.
Net Carbs: 16 gm.
Fat: 3 gm.
Sugar: 3 gm.
Calories: 112

What you need:

- 4 dinner rolls
- 1 cup your favorite cheese, grated
- 4 tbsp. butter, melted
- 1 clove garlic, chopped

Steps:

1. Set the air fryer to heat at a temperature of 350°F.
2. Blend the butter and garlic in a saucepan and remove from the burner after approximately 2 minutes to cool.
3. Slice the tops of the rolls to create a large hollow.
4. Equally, divide the cheese between the rolls and pack into the indentions.
5. Brush the garlic butter on each roll, covering as much as possible.
6. Transfer to the air fryer basket and steam for approximately 5 minutes.
7. Remove and enjoy immediately while hot.

Hush Puppies

Total Prep & Cooking Time: 30 minutes
Makes: 12 Hush Puppies
Protein: 2 gm.
Net Carbs: 16 gm.
Fat: 3 gm.
Sugar: 3 gm.
Calories: 112

What you need:

- one egg, preferably large
- all-purpose flour - 3/4 cup
- cornmeal - 8 oz.
- baking powder - 1 1/2 tsp.
- onion - 2 oz., chopped
- salt - 1/2 tsp.
- milk - 3/4 cup
- sugar - 1/4 tsp.
- cooking spray (olive oil)

Steps:

1. Insert a section of tin foil on the bottom of the basket of the air fryer.
2. Blend the sugar, baking powder, flour, cornmeal, and salt in a glass dish until incorporated.
3. Combine the egg, chopped onion and milk into the batter and integrate well.
4. Section the dough into 12 equal portions by using a cookie scooper.
5. Create mounds out of each section and transfer to the air fryer basket.
6. Coat the hush puppies with cooking spray (olive oil) and heat for 10 minutes at a temperature of 390°F.
7. Open the lid and carefully flip the hush puppies over. Spray an additional time with olive oil spray and continue to fry for another 10 minutes.
8. Remove and enjoy immediately while hot.

Monkey Bread

Total Prep & Cooking Time: 15 minutes
Makes: 8 Rolls
Protein: 1 gm.
Net Carbs: 6 gm.
Fat: 8 gm.
Sugar: 2 gm.
Calories: 110

What you need:

- self-rising flour - 8 oz.
- Sugar - 1 tsp., granulated
- non-fat Greek yogurt - 8 oz.
- cooking spray (olive oil)
- ground cinnamon - 1/2 tsp.

Steps:

1. Using a glass dish, blend the flour and yogurt for approximately 2 minutes until it becomes a thick dough.
2. Section into 8 equal portions and form into small mounds rolling by hand.
3. Empty the cinnamon and sugar into a ziplock bag and shake the balls in the mixture until fully coated.
4. Coat the base and inside of a mini bread pan with the cooking spray (olive oil) and press the dough balls together inside.
5. Dust with the desired amount of the remaining sugar and cinnamon mix and heat at 375°F for about 7 minutes.
6. Remove from the air fryer and wait approximately 5 minutes before serving hot.

Potato Stuffed Bread Rolls

Total Prep & Cooking Time: 1 hour 20 minutes
Makes: 8 Rolls, 4 Helpings
Protein: 24 gm.
Net Carbs: 6 gm.
Fat: 26 gm.
Sugar: 1 gm.
Calories: 192

What you need:

- 1 cup coriander, chopped finely
- 2 small onions, chopped finely
- 5 large russet potatoes
- 1/2 tsp. turmeric seasoning
- 2 sprigs curry leaves
- 8 1/2 cups water, separated
- 2 1/2 tbsp. cooking oil, separated
- 1 1/4 tsp. salt, separated
- 8 slices bread, crusts removed
- 1/2 tsp. mustard seeds
- 2 jalapeno, seeded and chopped finely

Steps:

1. Use a vegetable knife to peel the skins off the potatoes.
2. Warm a stewpot with 1 teaspoon of salt and 8 cups of the water. Once bubbling, adjust the heat to the medium setting.
3. Transfer the skinned potatoes to the pot and cover with a top. Steam the russet potatoes for approximately 15 minutes when they will be tender and remove from the burner.
4. Drain the water thoroughly and crush the potatoes completely with a masher.
5. Dissolve 1 tbsp. of the cooking oil in a hot pan and empty the mustard seeds into the pan. Blend the chopped onions into the skillet after approximately 20 seconds.
6. Sauté the onions for about 90 seconds and combine the curry leaves and turmeric into the pan.
7. Promptly distribute the mashed potatoes to the skillet and blend the remaining 1/4 teaspoon of salt.

8. Keep over the heat, occasionally stirring for about 60 seconds and remove from the burner.
9. After approximately 10 minutes, divide the potatoes into 8 sections.
10. Form oval rolls from each of the sections by hand and set to the side on a piece of baking lining.
11. Adjust the air fryer to the temperature of 390°F. Grease the inside of the basket with 1/2 tablespoon of cooking oil.
12. Using a glass dish, empty the remaining 1/2 cup of water on top of the crust-less bread.
13. Squeeze the individual slices of bread between your hands, keeping the bread flat, to remove as much moisture as possible from the bread.
14. Transfer one tablespoon of potato filler inside the moist bread and rotate the bread around to enclose the filling totally while pinching the sides. Place on the piece of baking lining.
15. Repeat steps 17 and 18 for all 8 rolls.
16. Apply the remaining tablespoon of cooking oil on top of the rolls.
17. Arrange the rolls in the basket, so there is room for the air to circulate and heat for approximately 12 minutes.
18. Remove from the air fryer to a serving plate. Serve hot after about 10 minutes.

Helpful Tip:
- You can get creative with this recipe and substitute any filling into these rolls such as vegetables or meat.

Pull-Apart Rolls

Total Prep & Cooking Time: 1 hour
Makes: 6 Rolls
Protein: 3 gm.
Net Carbs: 19 gm.
Fat: 2 gm.
Sugar: 4 gm.
Calories: 120

What you need:

- yeast - 1 1/4 tsp.
- olive oil - 3 tsp.
- butter - 5 1/4 tbsp.
- pepper - 1/8 tsp.
- all-purpose flour - 2 cups
- whole milk - 1 1/8 cups
- coconut oil - 3 tsp.
- salt - 1/4 tsp.

Steps:

1. Pulse the flour and butter in a food blender for about 45 seconds until completely combined.
2. Blend the coconut oil, milk, and olive oil in a hot skillet for approximately 90 seconds and empty into the food blender.
3. Combine the yeast and completely integrate the dough by hand until it thickens for about 5 minutes.
4. Transfer to the air fryer set at a temperature of 140°F and heat for 15 minutes.
5. Transfer the dough from the basket and knead it for approximately 10 minutes.
6. Equally, section the dough into 6 portions and roll into a mound.
7. Arrange the bread balls so they are all touching into the basket. You do not need a separate baking pan.
8. Set the temperature of the air fryer to 365°F for approximately 15 minutes and remove the rolls to a serving plate.
9. Serve hot and enjoy!

Helpful Tips:
- You may use your oven if your air fryer does not go as low as 140°F for 20 minutes.
- This dough recipe can be used for any type of bread or rolls that you would like to make including loaves.

Pumpkin Bread

Total Prep & Cooking Time: 45 minutes
Makes: 6 Slices
Protein: 3 gm.
Net Carbs: 37 gm.
Fat: 5 gm.
Sugar: 19 gm.
Calories: 140

What you need:

- ground cinnamon - 1 tsp.
- sugar - 3 cups, granulated
- baking powder - 1 tsp.
- pumpkin puree - 15 oz. can
- baking soda - 1 tsp.
- olive oil - 8 oz.
- ground cloves - 1 tsp.
- all-purpose flour - 3 cups
- salt - 1 tsp.
- three eggs, large
- cooking spray (olive oil)

Steps:

1. Use a food blender to pulse the pumpkin puree, flour, salt, and eggs for about 60 seconds.
2. Combine the ground cinnamon, baking powder, sugar and canola oil and pulse for one more minute.
3. Finally, blend the ground cloves and baking soda into the batter for another 15 seconds until completely combined.
4. Cover the side and base of the pan with the olive oil spray.
5. Empty the batter into the prepped pan and adjust the air fryer to the temperature of 350°F.
6. Heat the bread for 35 minutes and remove from the air fryer.
7. Wait approximately 10 minutes before slicing and serving warm.

Chapter 5: Appetizer & Side Recipes

Finding this cookbook easy to use with a variety of useful recipes? I would appreciate your feedback in a review on Amazon.

Bacon Brussels Sprouts

Total Prep & Cooking Time: 45 minutes
Makes: 6 Helpings
Protein: 5 gm.
Net Carbs: 6 gm.
Fat: 2 gm.
Sugar: 3 gm.
Calories: 100

What you need:

- 1/2 lb. bacon
- 16 oz. brussels sprouts, cut in half
- 6 tsp. avocado oil
- 1/2tsp. garlic powder
- 6 tsp. lime juice
- 1 tsp. mint leaves, garnish
- 2 oz. pistachios
- 1 1/4 tsp. salt, separated
- 5 dates, pitted and diced
- 1 tsp. basil leaves, garnish
- 4 tsp. lime juice, separated
- 1/8 tsp. pepper

Steps:

1. Brown the bacon in a frying pan for about 3 minutes and set on a plate covered with paper towels.
2. In a glass dish, coat the brussels sprouts with 3 teaspoons of the lime juice, one teaspoon of salt, avocado oil, and garlic powder until completely covered.
3. Transfer to the air fryer basket with the temperature set

61

to the 385°F.

4. Heat for a total of 25 minutes while tossing the brussels sprouts approximately every 5 minutes.

5. Crumble the bacon into a glass dish and set to the side.

6. At the 15 minute mark, combine the crumbled bacon, dates and pistachios into the basket of brussels sprouts and continue to cook for the remaining 10 minutes.

7. Remove and transfer the brussels sprouts to a serving platter and drizzle the remaining teaspoon of lime juice over the dish.

8. Dust the remaining 1/4 teaspoon of salt and pepper over the dish and garnish with the basil and mint leaves.

9. Serve right away and enjoy!

Blooming Onion

Total Prep & Cooking Time: 30 minutes
Makes: 2 Helpings
Protein: 9 gm.
Net Carbs: 40 gm.
Fat: 3 gm.
Sugar: 10 gm.
Calories: 221

What you need:

- one large onion, sweet
- salt - 3 tsp.
- cayenne pepper - 1 /2 tsp.
- cooking spray (olive oil)
- garlic powder - 1 tsp.
- milk - 4 oz.
- one large egg
- all-purpose flour - 4 oz.
- olive oil - 1/2 tsp.

Steps:

1. You will need to prepare a piece of tin foil on top of a cutting board.
2. Brush 1/2 teaspoon of olive oil onto the center of the foil.
3. Slice the top half-inch of the onion off and remove the outer skin of the onion entirely.
4. Slice the onion in half, stopping half an inch above the root.
5. Make a similar cut perpendicular to the first, creating 4 sections of sliced onion.
6. Continue to cut the onion using this method and finish the cuts once there are 16 sections of onion slices.
7. Adjust the air fryer temperature to 370°F to heat.
8. Whip the cayenne pepper, garlic powder, flour, and salt in a glass dish with a whisk to remove all lumpiness.
9. Using another bowl, blend the egg and milk until combined.
10. Immerse the onion slices in the eggs ensuring they are completely coated.
11. Repeat by coating completely in the seasoned flour and spoon over each section to make sure no area is missed.

Shake thoroughly to remove extra flour by turning upside down.

12. Apply the cooking oil onto each section of the onion and transfer to the air fryer basket.
13. Heat for approximately 10 minutes and remove if the crust is golden. If not, cook for an additional 5 minutes.
14. Serve immediately.

Helpful Tip:
- It is very important to leave half an inch uncut at the root of the onion. Otherwise, the sections of the onion will come apart during preparation.

Bok Choy Salad

Total Prep & Cooking Time: 10 minutes
Makes: 2 Helpings
Protein: 1 gm.
Net Carbs: 3 gm.
Fat: 0 gm.
Sugar: 0 gm.
Calories: 13

What you need:

- 1/2 tsp. sesame seeds, toasted
- 2 heads baby bok choy, halved
- 1 tbsp. toasted sesame oil
- 2 oz. shiitake mushrooms, stemmed
- 1/4 tsp. salt

Steps:

1. Adjust the temperature of the air fryer to 400°F.
2. Slice the stems off the mushrooms and chop the bok choy in halves.
3. Apply sesame oil by brushing over the mushrooms and bok choy. Dust with salt and transfer to the air fryer basket.
4. Set for 5 minutes and remove to a plate. Drizzle the sesame seeds over the dish and enjoy while hot.

Cheesy Ravioli

Total Prep & Cooking Time: 25 minutes
Makes: 15 Pieces
Protein: 8 gm.
Net Carbs: 33 gm.
Fat: 3 gm.
Sugar: 4 gm.
Calories: 215

What you need:

- prepackaged ravioli - 16 oz., frozen
- bread crumbs - 1 cup
- garlic powder - 3 tsp.
- parmesan cheese - 1/2 cup
- two eggs, preferably large
- Italian seasoning - 1 tbs.
- cooking spray (olive oil)

Steps:

1. Blend the parmesan cheese, Italian seasoning, garlic powder, breadcrumbs in a glass dish.
2. Whisk the eggs in another bowl and set to the side.
3. Coat the basket of the air fryer with olive oil spray.
4. Immerse the frozen ravioli pieces into the egg making sure they are covered completely.
5. Coat the ravioli in the flour and transfer to the air fryer basket when breaded.
6. Adjust the air fryer temperature to 350°F and heat for a total of 15 minutes.
7. At the 8 minute mark, toss the ravioli to ensure they will fully cook.
8. Remove and empty onto a serving plate and enjoy immediately.

Chicken Wings

Total Prep & Cooking Time: 30 minutes
Makes: 4 Helpings
Protein: 22 gm.
Net Carbs: 22 gm.
Fat: 19 gm.
Sugar: 17 gm.
Calories: 365

What you need:

- pepper - 1 tsp.
- chicken wings - 2 lbs.
- salt - 1 tsp.
- sauce of your choice -3/4 cup
- parsley seasoning - 1 tbsp.

Steps:

1. Using paper towels, remove the excess moisture from the chicken. Sprinkle with the pepper and salt.
2. Arrange the wings in the basket of the air fryer in a single layer so they do not touch.
3. Heat for 10 minutes at a temperature of 400°F.
4. Flip the chicken and continue to fry for an additional 10 minutes.
5. Use a meat thermometer to ensure the chicken is cooked to 160°F before removing to a glass dish.
6. Empty the sauce you have chosen over the chicken and coat the chicken completely using a rubber spatula to toss.
7. Grill the chicken once again in the air fryer at the same temperature for an additional 5 minutes.
8. Remove to a plate, sprinkle the parsley over the dish and enjoy hot!

Edamame

Total Prep & Cooking Time: 10 minutes
Makes: 4 Helpings
Protein: 2 gm.
Net Carbs: 1 gm.
Fat: 1 gm.
Sugar: 0 gm.
Calories: 30

What you need:

- 1 tsp. avocado oil
- 16 oz. Edamame, unshelled and frozen

Steps:

1. Drizzle the avocado oil over a dish containing the edamame and toss to coat completely.
2. Adjust the air fryer temperature to heat at 390°F for approximately 10 minutes.
3. At the 5 minute mark, stir the edamame.
4. Remove to a serving dish and enjoy while warm.

Helpful Tips:
- The edible part of edamame is the beans inside of the pods. It is not advisable to eat the pod, although you can if you prefer.

Eggplant Parmesan

Total Prep & Cooking Time: 45 minutes
Makes: 4 Helpings
Protein: 8 gm.
Net Carbs: 8 gm.
Fat: 4 gm.
Sugar: 8 gm.
Calories: 126

What you need:

- eggplant - 1 1/4 lb.
- all-purpose flour - 3 tbsp.
- parsley - 1 tbsp., chopped
- bread crumbs - 4 oz.
- basil - 1 tbsp., chopped
- parmesan cheese - 3 tbsp., grated finely
- Italian seasoning - 1 tsp.
- cooking spray (olive oil)
- salt - 1/4 tsp.
- marinara sauce - 8 oz.
- mozzarella cheese - 1/4 cup, grated
- one egg white, large
- water - 1 tbsp.

Steps:

1. Slice the eggplant into half-inch rounds and sprinkle salt on either side. Transfer to a baking lining covered flat sheet and set aside for approximately 15 minutes.
2. In the meantime, blend the water, flour and egg white in a glass dish.
3. In a separate dish, toss the parmesan cheese, breadcrumbs, salt, and Italian seasoning until thoroughly integrated.
4. Adjust the temperature of the air fryer to heat at 360°F.
5. Using a fork to hold the individual eggplant slices, dunk into the dish with the egg and then the breadcrumbs, making sure not to over bread. Transfer back to the baking sheet.
6. Apply the cooking spray (olive oil) over the eggplant slices and arrange greased side down on a wire rack placed inside the air fryer basket.

7. Steam for about 8 minutes and open the lid.
8. Spread approximately a tablespoon of marinara sauce on each eggplant slice.
9. Divide the mozzarella cheese evenly and sprinkle on top of each serving of eggplant.
10. Heat for another 2 minutes and enjoy immediately while hot.

French Fries

Total Prep & Cooking Time: 30 minutes
Makes: 4 Helpings
Protein: 3 gm.
Net Carbs: 24 gm.
Fat: 7 gm.
Sugar: 1 gm.
Calories: 170

What you need:

- salt - 1/4 tsp.
- olive oil - 2 tsp.
- garlic powder - 1/4 tsp.
- potatoes - 1 lb.
- pepper - 1/4 tsp.

Steps:

1. Scrub the potatoes and remove the skins with a vegetable peeler if you prefer.
2. Slice the potatoes into long quarter-inch sections and place into a glass dish.
3. Using a rubber scraper, blend the salt, olive oil, garlic powder, and pepper over the potatoes, evenly coating.
4. Evenly arrange the fries in the basket of the fryer, keeping them 2 layers or less.
5. Heat the air fryer for approximately 20 minutes at a temperature of 380°F.
6. At the 10 minute mark, toss the fries gently and continue to broil for the remaining 10 minutes.
7. Empty the basket onto a plate and serve immediately.

Helpful Tip:
- If you like to have crispy fries, toss the potatoes again after cooking for 20 minutes. Then continue to fry for another 3 minutes.

Fried Green Tomatoes

Total Prep & Cooking Time: 20 minutes
Makes: 4 Helpings
Protein: 1 gm.
Net Carbs: 14 gm.
Fat: 7 gm.
Sugar: 3 gm.
Calories: 128

What you need:

- Buttermilk - 1/2 cup
- Two green tomatoes, medium
- salt - 1/2 tsp., separated
- two large eggs
- pepper - 1/4 tsp.
- panko bread crumbs - 8 oz.
- cornmeal - 1 cup
- all-purpose flour - 4 oz.
- cooking spray (olive oil)

Steps:

1. Chop the tomatoes into quarter-inch slices and use paper towels to remove the moisture.
2. Dust with the pepper and 1/4 teaspoon of salt on both sides and set to the side on a plate.
3. Empty the flour into a glass dish. In an additional dish, whip the buttermilk and eggs until combined.
4. In a third dish, blend the cornmeal and breadcrumbs.
5. Adjust the temperature of the air fryer to heat at 400°F.
6. Cover the slices of tomato firstly in the flour and then the egg, removing the excess.
7. Compress the tomato slices into the breadcrumbs on either side to help the crumbs to stick properly. Dust the tomatoes with the remaining 1/4 teaspoon of salt.
8. Coat the basket of the air fryer with the cooking spray and transfer the slices inside.
9. Apply a layer of cooking spray (olive oil) to the top of the

    tomatoes and close the lid.

10. Set the timer for five minutes and then turn the slices over.
11. Use the cooking spray (olive oil) to apply another coat to the tomatoes and continue to fry for an additional 3 minutes.
12. Serve immediately and enjoy while hot.

Fried Mushrooms

Total Prep & Cooking Time: 15 minutes
Makes: 4 Helpings
Protein: 0 gm.
Net Carbs: 0 gm.
Fat: 4 gm.
Sugar: 0 gm.
Calories: 44

What you need:

- Salt - 3/4 tbsp.
- baby portobello mushrooms - 1 lb.
- garlic powder - 3/4 tsp.
- two eggs, large
- onion powder - 3/4 tsp.
- 1 tsp. creole seasoning, separated
- cooking spray (olive oil)
- panko bread crumbs - 1 cup
- pepper - 3/4 tsp.
- all-purpose flour - 1 cup
- paprika seasoning - 3/4 tsp.

Steps:

1. Clean the portabella mushrooms by removing any dirt and slice into 4 sections.
2. In a glass dish, whip the eggs and blend with 1/4 teaspoon of the creole seasoning.
3. Empty the flour, garlic powder, salt, breadcrumbs, onion powder, pepper, paprika seasoning, and the remaining 3/4 teaspoon of the creole seasoning into a large ziplock bag. Shake until combined and set to the side.
4. Transfer the sections of mushrooms in stages to the egg mixture. Once fully coated, shake to remove the excess egg.
5. Transfer to the ziplock bag and agitate to coat the mushrooms completely in the breading.
6. Remove the mushrooms from the bag and distribute to the basket of the air fryer, leaving space in between.
7. Coat the mushrooms generously with the cooking spray.

Shake the basket and spray the mushrooms on the other side with the cooking spray (olive oil).

8. Adjust the temperature of the air fryer to 400°F and heat for 3 minutes.
9. Open the lid and agitate the basket. Fry for an additional 4 minutes.
10. Transfer the mushrooms from the air fryer to a serving plate.
11. Repeat steps 6 through 10 as necessary.
12. Serve and enjoy immediately.

Helpful Tip:
- You can also use white button mushrooms in place of the baby portabella mushrooms.

Fried Okra

Total Prep & Cooking Time: 20 minutes
Makes: 4 Helpings
Protein: 6 gm.
Net Carbs: 10 gm.
Fat: 2 gm.
Sugar: 0 gm.
Calories: 63

What you need:

- one large egg
- salt - 1/2 tsp.
- okra - 2 1/2 cups
- all-purpose flour - 1 cup
- paprika seasoning - 1/2 tsp.
- cooking spray (olive oil)
- pepper - 1/2 tsp.

Steps:

1. In a glass dish, whip the egg and blend with half the pepper and salt.
2. Empty the flour, paprika and the remaining 1/4 teaspoon of pepper and salt into a large ziplock bag. Shake until blended and set to the side.
3. Scrub the okra and dry using several paper towels to remove any moisture.
4. Remove both the ends of each piece of okra with a knife and discard.
5. Chop the okra into half-inch pieces.
6. Transfer the sliced okra in batches to the egg mixture. Once coated, transfer to the ziplock bag using a slotted spoon.
7. Agitate the ziplock bag to coat the okra completely in the breading.
8. Remove the okra from the bag and distribute to the basket of the air fryer.
9. Spray the okra with the olive oil.
10. Adjust the temperature of the air fryer to 400°F and heat for 4 minutes.
11. Open the lid and agitate the basket. Spray with olive oil

once again. Fry for an additional 4 minutes.
12. Transfer the fried okra from the air fryer to a serving plate.
13. Serve and enjoy immediately.

Fried Pickles

Total Prep & Cooking Time: 20 minutes
Makes: 4 Helpings
Protein: 3 gm.
Net Carbs: 2 gm.
Fat: 2 gm.
Sugar: 0 gm.
Calories: 48

What you need:

- panko bread crumbs - 1/3 cup
- jar dill pickles - 16 oz., whole
- one egg, large
- dill weed - 1/8 tsp.
- grated Parmesan - 2 tbsp.

Steps:

1. Drain the pickles from the jar and cut diagonally to be quarter-inch thick slices.
2. Transfer to a few sections of paper towels to remove all the fluid. Set to the side.
3. Whip the egg in a glass dish and set aside.
4. Use a ziplock bag to shake the parmesan, dill weed, and bread crumbs until combined.
5. Immerse the chips in small quantities into the egg and shake to remove the extra fluid.
6. Transfer to the ziplock bag and shake until the chips are fully coated.
7. Move to the air fry basket and put no more than 2 layers of pickles in the basket. Repeat steps 5 through 8 for a second batch if necessary.
8. At a temperature of 400°F, heat the pickles for 9 minutes.
9. Remove and serve immediately.

Helpful Tip:
- This recipe is unique in that you do not need to agitate the basket halfway through.
- If you want to ensure the breading does not fall off, you can refrigerate the pickles after step 4 for approximately half an hour.
- You may also substitute pre-sliced pickles for the dill pickles.

Grilled Pineapple

Total Prep & Cooking Time: 20 minutes
Makes: 4 Helpings
Protein: 1 gm.
Net Carbs: 54 gm.
Fat: 8 gm.
Sugar: 48 gm.
Calories: 295

What you need:

- butter - 3 tbsp.
- one small pineapple
- ground cinnamon - 2 tsp.
- brown sugar - 1/2 cup

Steps:

1. Dissolve the butter in a saucepan and empty into a glass dish.
2. Blend the cinnamon and brown sugar with the melted butter until combined. Set to the side.
3. Prepare the pineapple by cutting off the top and removing the outside completely.
4. Slice into several one-inch wide wedges.
5. Apply the sweetened butter to the sliced pineapple using a pastry brush and holding the pineapple with a pair of tongs. Alternatively, you can place them on a sheet of baking lining and apply the butter to one side. Then flip over the pineapple to apply butter to the other side.
6. Transfer the coated pineapple to the basket of the air fryer in a single layer.
7. Heat for 10 minutes at a temperature of 400°F.
8. At the halfway mark, open the lid and apply the remaining butter to the pineapple.
9. Remove the pineapple from the basket. It should have bubbling sugar on top.
10. Enjoy immediately.

Helpful Tip:
- If you have a smaller air fryer, you may need to do another batch. If this is the case, set the timer for only 7 minutes as the fryer will already be heated.

Kale Chips

Total Prep & Cooking Time: 15 minutes
Makes: 2 Helpings
Protein: 1 gm.
Net Carbs: 5 gm.
Fat: 2 gm.
Sugar: 0 gm.
Calories: 20

What you need:

- salt - 1/4 tsp.
- kale - 3 cups
- cooking spray (avocado oil)
- pepper - 1/8 tsp.
- chili powder - 1/4 tsp.

Steps:

1. Remove the hard stems and tear the kale into smaller bite-sized pieces.
2. Place the kale into the air fryer basket and coat with the avocado oil cooking spray. Toss to cover the kale evenly.
3. Sprinkle the salt, chili pepper, and pepper into the basket and shake again to coat the kale.
4. Heat for approximately 7 minutes at a temperature of 375°F.
5. Agitate the basket about every couple of minutes to make sure the kale does not stick.
6. Remove to a serving plate and serve hot.

Helpful Tip:
- You may use fresh kale or prepackaged for this recipe.

Mozzarella Sticks

Total Prep & Cooking Time: 30 minutes
Makes: 12 Sticks
Protein: 3 gm.
Net Carbs: 2 gm.
Fat: 2 gm.
Sugar: 0 gm.
Calories: 48

What you need:

- onion powder - ½ tsp.
- mozzarella string cheese - 5 oz.
- garlic powder - ½ tsp.
- cooking spray (olive oil)
- one egg, large
- salt - 1/2tsp.
- panko breadcrumbs - 2 oz.
- chili powder – 1/2
- all-purpose flour - 2 tbsp.
- paprika powder - 1/2tsp.

Steps:

1. Cut the mozzarella sticks in halves and transfer to a freezer safe zip lock bag. Freeze for approximately half an hour.
2. Whip the egg in a glass dish and set to the side.
3. Completely blend the garlic powder, breadcrumbs, salt, chili powder, paprika powder, and onion powder until integrated fully in a separate dish.
4. Prepare a flat sheet layered with baking lining.
5. Use another ziplock bag to combine the flour and mozzarella cheese by shaking until the cheese is covered fully.
6. Remove the cheese from the ziplock bag and dip into the egg fully and secondly into the breadcrumbs until completely covered.
7. Set on the prepped sheet and repeat for the other mozzarella sticks.
8. Freeze the cheese for approximately 60 minutes.

9. Adjust the temperature of the air fryer to 370°F to heat.
10. Coat the inside basket of the air fryer with the olive oil.
11. Remove the cheese from the freezer. Transfer 6 sticks to the air fryer basket and arrange so they are not touching.
12. Steam for approximately 5 minutes, remove to a serving platter and place the remaining cheese sticks into the air fryer basket for approximately 5 additional minutes.
13. Serve immediately with a dipping sauce of your choice or enjoy as is.

Nacho Chips

Total Prep & Cooking Time: 30 minutes
Makes: 4 Helpings
Protein: 2 gm.
Net Carbs: 16 gm.
Fat: 4 gm.
Sugar: 0 gm.
Calories: 130

What you need:

- salt - 1/4 tsp.
- sweet corn - 1/2 cup
- all-purpose flour - 8 oz.
- chili powder - 1/2 tsp.
- all-purpose flour - 2 oz., separate
- water - 2 tsp.
- butter - 3 tsp.

Steps:

1. In a food blender, whip the sweet corn and water into a smooth paste.
2. Combine the salt, chili powder, 8 ounces of flour, and butter and pulse until it becomes thick dough.
3. Dust the counter with the remaining 2 ounces of flour and flatten the dough with the use of a rolling pin until the desired thinness for the chips is achieved.
4. Slice into separate chips to your preferred size and shape.
5. Transfer the chips to the basket and heat for approximately 7 minutes.
6. Remove and serve with your favorite dip or salsa.

Onion Rings

Total Prep & Cooking Time: 1 hour 20 minutes
Makes: 4 Helpings
Protein: 20 gm.
Net Carbs: 79 gm.
Fat: 8 gm.
Sugar: 6 gm.
Calories: 506

What you need:

- two eggs, preferably large
- red onion - 13 oz.
- salt - 3/4 tbsp.
- cooking spray (olive oil)
- all-purpose flour - 2 cups
- pepper - 3 tsp.
- panko breadcrumbs - 2 1/2 cups

Steps:

1. Remove the outer layer off the onion and chop into thick ¾-inch slices. Take the rings out of the individual slices. Set to the side.
2. Create a dredging station with three glass dishes.
3. In the first dish, whip the eggs until smooth. In the second dish, empty the flour, and the third will contain the breadcrumbs.
4. Blend 1 teaspoon of pepper and 1/4 tablespoon of salt into each of the dishes and combine well.
5. Use a fork to immerse the rings individually into the egg dish and then the flour, repeating the process for finally covering with the breadcrumbs. Compress the breadcrumbs as necessary to help them to stick.
6. Make sure that each ring is covered fully but shake in between to remove the excess.
7. Place on a baking lining covered flat sheet and freeze for approximately 30 minutes.
8. Adjust the air fryer temperature to heat at 375°F.
9. Take the onions out of the freezer and transfer to the air fryer basket in a single layer.

10. Coat lightly with the cooking spray and fry for a total of approximately 12 minutes.
11. At approximately 6 minutes into frying, flip the rings over to the other side and spray again with the cooking spray.
12. Remove and enjoy hot.

Helpful Tips:

- You can pre-make these onion rings and freeze for up to 7 days.

- Alternatively, you can substitute other types of onions including Vidalia, Spanish or sweet onions. Avoid the yellow onions for this recipe.

Pigs in a Blanket Minis

Total Prep & Cooking Time: 45 minutes
Makes: 8 Pigs in a Blanket, 4 Helpings
Protein: 2 gm.
Net Carbs: 7 gm.
Fat: 2 gm.
Sugar: 0 gm.
Calories: 46

What you need:

- 4 oz. can refrigerated crescent rolls
- 8 smoked sausages, mini

Steps:

1. Remove the moisture from the sausages by soaking up the water with paper towels. Set to the side.
2. Open the crescent roll can and flatten the dough on a piece of baking lining.
3. Cut the triangles into two equal pieces leaving you with 8 separate slices of dough.
4. Set a mini sausage at the longest section of the dough and rotate the dough to encase the sausage fully. Repeat this step for all the sausage links.
5. Transfer to the basket of the air fryer and heat at a temperature of 330°F for approximately 8 minutes.
6. Remove and enjoy as is or with your favorite sauce or dip.

Potato Chips

Total Prep & Cooking Time: 20 minutes
Makes: 4 Helpings
Protein: 4 gm.
Net Carbs: 17 gm.
Fat: 2 gm.
Sugar: 3 gm.
Calories: 86

What you need:

- 1 large russet potato
- cooking spray (olive oil)
- 3/4 tbsp. salt

Steps:

1. Use a cheese grater or a kitchen mandolin to cut the potato into at least ¼-inch thin slices. If you can, make them as thin as 1/16-inch thin.
2. Soak up the moisture in the chips with several paper towels.
3. Coat the air fryer basket with the cooking spray (olive oil) and arrange a single layer of potato chips inside.
4. Lightly apply the top of the chips with additional cooking spray (olive oil).
5. Heat at a temperature of 450°F for approximately 15 minutes.
6. Remove to the counter on a platter and repeat steps 9 through 11 until all chips are complete.

Helpful Tip:
- The chips will get crisper if you leave them overnight on the counter.
- If you want to flavor your chips, dust the seasonings of your choice on the chips after you have sprayed with the cooking oil. If you want them to be completely coated in flavor, toss the chips in a bowl with 1 tsp. of oil with the spices before transferring to the air fryer basket.

Pretzel Poppers

Total Prep & Cooking Time: 45 minutes
Makes: 5 Helpings
Protein: 1 gm.
Net Carbs: 3 gm.
Fat: 2 gm.
Sugar: 1 gm.
Calories: 25

What you need:

- Water - 4 cups
- butter - 2 tbsp., unsalted
- four-count refrigerated buttermilk biscuits
- garlic powder - 1/4 tsp.
- cooking spray (olive oil)
- baking soda - 1/4 cup
- sea salt - 1 tbsp.

Steps:

1. Prepare a flat sheet with a rim covered with baking lining. Set to the side.
2. Warm the baking soda and water in a big pot, bringing to a simmer.
3. Open the can of biscuits and slice into quarters, making a total of 20 pieces.
4. Create small balls and transfer to the simmering water for 2 minutes while occasionally stirring.
5. With a slotted spoon, scoop out the cooked balls and move to the prepped flat sheet. Let them cool for approximately 10 minutes.
6. In the meantime, liquefy the butter in a saucepan. Empty into a dish to combine with the garlic powder until integrated.
7. Adjust the air fryer temperature to 400°F.
8. Spread the spiced butter on each pretzel with a pastry brush.
9. Arrange the pretzels inside the basket in a single layer. Make sure there is space in between each ball. You will most likely need to fry in stages.

10. Set the timer for 10 minutes and turn the pretzels over at the halfway mark.
11. Remove to a serving plate and dust with the sea salt.
12. Repeat steps 15 through 17 until all pretzel bites are complete and enjoy!

Helpful Tips:
- Avoid using the flaky type of refrigerated biscuits in this recipe, as they will not stay in a uniform ball.

Rib Bites

Total Prep & Cooking Time: 25 minutes in addition to 2 hours of marinating time
Makes: 4 Helpings
Protein: 3 gm.
Net Carbs: 2 gm.
Fat: 2 gm.
Sugar: 0 gm.
Calories: 48

What you need:

- pork riblets - 1 lb.
- soy sauce - 2 1/3 tbsp.
- dry sherry - 3 tbsp.
- sugar - 1 1/2 tbsp., granulated
- garlic - 6 large cloves, peeled and halved
- oyster sauce - 1 tbsp.

Steps:

1. Slice the ribs into small half-inch pieces with the bone intact and transfer to a big lidded tub.
2. Blend the soy sauce, oyster sauce, dry sherry, sugar and halved cloves of garlic into the tub.
3. Cover the ribs completely in the fluid.
4. Refrigerate for a minimum of 2 hours if not overnight to marinate.
5. When the meat is marinated, heat the air fryer to the temperature of 360°F.
6. Remove the marinade from the fridge and drain extremely well.
7. Arrange the rib bites in a single layer in the basket of the air fryer, allowing for a room in between.
8. Fry for a total of 12 minutes while flipping the ribs at the halfway mark.
9. Remove to a platter and enjoy immediately.

Roasted Asparagus

Total Prep & Cooking Time: 10 minutes
Makes: 4 Helpings
Protein: 4 gm.
Net Carbs: 2 gm.
Fat: 4 gm.
Sugar: 0 gm.
Calories: 53

What you need:

- pepper - 1/8 tsp.
- extra virgin olive oil - 1 tbsp.
- salt - 1/8 tsp.
- asparagus - 1 lb.

Steps:

1. Slice the last inch of the base of the vegetables off and toss in the trash.
2. Transfer the cut asparagus into a dish. Empty the oil completely over the dish. Dust with pepper and salt.
3. Use a rubber scraper to cover the seasoning and oil over the asparagus completely.
4. Empty the asparagus into the air fryer basket and close the lid. Heat for 7 minutes at a temperature of 400°F.
5. Remove to a serving platter and immediately enjoy.

Roasted Garlic Potatoes

Total Prep & Cooking Time: 40 minutes
Makes: 6 Helpings
Protein: 1 gm.
Net Carbs: 54 gm.
Fat: 8 gm.
Sugar: 48 gm.
Calories: 295

What you need:

- oregano seasoning - 1/2 tsp.
- butter - 2 tbsp., unsalted
- pepper - 1/4 tsp.
- garlic - 5 cloves, minced
- basil seasoning - 1/2 tsp.
- red potatoes - 3 lbs.
- thyme seasoning - 1 tsp.
- olive oil - 2 tbsp.
- parmesan cheese - 1/3 cup, grated
- parsley leaves - 2 tbsp.
- salt - 1/4 tsp.

Steps:

1. Dissolve the butter in a hot pot and move away from the burner. Set to the side.
2. Thoroughly wash and scrub the potatoes and chop into 4 sections.
3. Use a ziplock bag to shake the basil, garlic, oregano, parsley leaves, salt, thyme, and pepper until thoroughly mixed.
4. Finally, blend the potatoes, melted butter, parmesan cheese and olive in the bag and agitate until the potatoes are entirely covered.
5. Cut a piece of baking lining to fit the base of the basket of the air fryer.
6. Empty the spiced potatoes into the basket and heat for approximately 20 minutes at a temperature of 400°F.
7. Stir the contents about 10 minutes into frying.
8. Remove to a serving dish and enjoy while hot.

Spiced Butternut Squash

Total Prep & Cooking Time: 30 minutes
Makes: 4 Helpings
Protein: 1 gm.
Net Carbs: 14 gm.
Fat: 7 gm.
Sugar: 3 gm.
Calories: 128

What you need:

- ground cloves - 1/4 tsp.
- ground cinnamon - 1 1/2 tsp.
- butternut squash - 4 cups, cubed
- ground nutmeg - 1/2 tsp.
- ground allspice - 1/4 tsp.
- brown sugar - 2 tbsp.
- ground ginger - 1/2 tsp.
- olive oil - 2 tbsp.

Steps:

1. Wash the butternut squash and chop into 1-inch cubes. Transfer to a glass dish.
2. Blend the brown sugar, cinnamon, nutmeg, allspice, cloves, ginger, and the olive oil until the squash is evenly covered.
3. Empty the dish into the air fryer basket. Adjust the temperature to 400°F and heat for about 15 minutes.
4. Shake the basket at the 8-minute mark and continue to cook until evenly browned.
5. Remove from the basket and enjoy immediately.

Sweet Potato Tots

Total Prep & Cooking Time: 25 minutes
Makes: 4 Helpings, 6 Tots per Helping
Protein: 1 gm.
Net Carbs: 13 gm.
Fat: 4 gm.
Sugar: 8 gm.
Calories: 100

What you need:

- 1/2 tsp. coriander seasoning
- 2 cups sweet potato puree
- 1/2 tsp. salt
- 4 oz. panko breadcrumbs
- 1/2 tsp. cumin seasoning
- olive oil cooking oil

Steps:

1. Prepare a baking lining covered flat sheet and set to the side.
2. In a big glass dish, blend the coriander, sweet potato puree, salt, breadcrumbs, and cumin until thoroughly combined.
3. Heat the air fryer to the temperature of 390°F.
4. Spoon out approximately one tablespoon of sweet potatoes and create the shape of tots that you prefer by hand.
5. There will be 24 individual tots when you are finished and transfer to the prepped flat sheet.
6. Apply the cooking spray (olive oil) to the top and roll them around to apply to the bottom as well.
7. Distribute the tots to the basket of the air fryer in a single layer leaving room in between.
8. Set the timer for approximately 7 minutes and turn the tots to the other side.
9. Continue to fry for an additional 5 minutes.
10. Repeat steps 18 through 20 for the remaining tots.
11. Enjoy immediately with your favorite sauce or dip.

Helpful Tip:

- When you go to turn the tots, if they are soft keep them in for an additional 3 minutes before attempting to flip again.
- You can prepare these tots up to 7 days in advance and freeze until you are prepared to eat them. Simply move them to a freezer safe zip lock bag after forming the tots and label with the date. To heat, after they have been frozen, adjust the air fryer to the same temperature and cook for 10 minutes before turning. Then continue to fry for another 5 minutes.

Zucchini Corn Fritters

Total Prep & Cooking Time: 35 minutes
Makes: 4 Helpings
Protein: 3 gm.
Net Carbs: 2 gm.
Fat: 2 gm.
Sugar: 0 gm.
Calories: 48

What you need:

- salt - 1/4 tsp.
- one medium potato cooked
- two medium zucchinis
- garlic - 1 clove, minced finely
- corn kernels - 8 oz.
- all-purpose flour - 2 tbsp.
- olive oil - 2 tsp.
- Pepper - 1/4 tsp.
- cold water - 3 cups

Steps:

1. Prepare a flat sheet by layering baking lining over the top. Set to the side.
2. Thoroughly wash and scrub the zucchini and potato.
3. Use a cheese grater to slice the zucchini using the largest holes and transfer to a glass dish.
4. Dust with 1/4 tsp. of the salt and let it sit for approximately 15 minutes.
5. In the meantime, nuke the potato for about 3 minutes in the microwave. Use oven mitts to remove to a glass dish with the cold water for approximately 5 minutes.
6. Remove the water from the bowl and use a vegetable peeler to remove the skins.
7. Replace the cooked potato in the glass dish and smash with a fork or masher.
8. Remove the extra moisture from the zucchini by twisting in a tea towel.

9. Using a food blender, pulse the zucchini, flour, salt, mashed potato, corn, and pepper for approximately 2 minutes until combined totally.
10. Adjust the temperature of the air fryer to heat at 360°F.
11. Spoon about 2 tablespoons of the batter and form into patties by hand.
12. Transfer the patties to the prepped flat sheet. Repeat until you have a total of 4 patties.
13. Apply the olive oil to the top of the patties using a pastry brush.
14. Arrange the patties in the air fryer basket, leaving space in between, and fry for 8 minutes.
15. Flip the patties over and continue to fry for approximately 4 additional minutes.
16. Repeat steps 19 and 20 if you could not fit the 4 patties in one time.
17. Serve while still hot and enjoy!

Helpful tips:
- Make sure that the zucchini is not bruised and is properly fresh and firm.
- You can easily use frozen or canned corn for this recipe.

Chapter 6: Dinner Recipes

Beef and Vegetable Stir Fry

Total Prep & Cooking Time: 50 minutes
Makes: 2 Helpings
Protein: 2 gm.
Net Carbs: 10 gm.
Fat: 7 gm.
Sugar: 0 gm.
Calories: 122

What you need:

For the stir-fry:
- one yellow pepper
- beef sirloin - 16 oz.
- one green pepper
- onion - 1/2 cup
- broccoli - 24 oz., florets
- one red pepper
- red onion - 1/2 cup
- 1 tbsp. olive oil

For the sauce:
- hoisin sauce - 1/4 cup
- sesame oil - 1 tsp.
- water - 1/4 cup
- soy sauce - 3 tsp.
- ground ginger - 1 tsp.
- garlic - 2 tsp.,
  minced

Steps:

1. Chop the peppers and onions into long strips and set to the side in a glass dish.
2. Slice the beef sirloin into strips approximately two inches long and set aside along with the vegetables.
3. In a lidded tub, blend the water, ground ginger, soy sauce, sesame oil, minced garlic, and hoisin sauce until thoroughly combined.
4. Transfer the sliced sirloin into the marinade and refrigerate for approximately 20 minutes.
5. About 10 minutes before you start cooking, heat the air fryer to the temperature of 200°F.
6. Drizzle the olive oil over the sliced vegetables and toss until covered.
7. Transfer the vegetables to the basket of the air fryer and fry for approximately 5 minutes.
8. Meanwhile, thoroughly drain the marinade from the sirloin.
9. Check the softness of the vegetables. If they are still hard, fry for another 2 minutes.
10. Transfer the air-fried vegetables to a glass bowl and adjust the temperature to 360°F.
11. Transfer the drained sirloin into the air fryer basket and heat for 4 minutes.
12. Flip the meat to the other side. Steam for approximately 2 minutes or to your desired level of doneness.
13. Remove to the same dish as the vegetables and serve immediately.

Beef Wellington

Total Prep & Cooking Time: 1 hour
Makes: 2 helpings
Protein: 23 gm.
Net Carbs: 4 gm.
Fat: 15 gm.
Sugar: 2 gm.
Calories: 250

What you need:

- beef fillet - 16 oz.
- salt - 1/4 tsp.
- olive oil - 1 tsp.
- puff pastry - 10 oz.
- liver pate - 3.50 oz.
- two egg yolks
- pepper- 1/4 tsp.

Steps:

1. Heat a skillet to be very warm. Divide the beef fillet into equal halves. Apply the olive oil to the beef fillets with a pastry brush and sear the meat for about 30 seconds.
2. Turn to the other side and fry for another 30 seconds.
3. Remove from the burner to a plate and set to the side.
4. Whip the egg yolks in a small dish and set to the side.
5. Slice 2 puff pastries to be approximately 4" longer than the length of the fillets.
6. Apply the liver pate over the fillets and arrange in the middle of the individual pastries.
7. Rotate the puff pastry over the fillets, completely encasing the meat.
8. Remove the excess pastry and close the ends by applying the egg yolks with a pastry brush. Compress the ends together to seal properly.
9. Continue to apply egg yolks to the open sections of the pastry and seal them by pressing on the ends.
10. Move the encased fillets to the grill tray. Coat the top of the pastries with additional egg yolk and store in the fridge for 20 minutes.

11. Adjust the temperature of the air fryer to 350°F and remove the pastries from the refrigerator.
12. Slice the tops of the pastries about 4 times so they pastries will properly cook.
13. Fry for half an hour and wait about 10 minutes before serving hot.

Chicken Parmesan

Total Prep & Cooking Time: 20 minutes
Makes: 4 Helpings
Protein: 24 gm.
Net Carbs: 6 gm.
Fat: 26 gm.
Sugar: 1 gm.
Calories: 192

What you need:

- Asiago cheese - 1/2 cup, grated
- 4 chicken breast paillards
- pepper - 1/3 tsp.
- one cup of milk
- panko bread crumbs - 4 oz.
- salt - 1/3 tsp.
- cooking spray (olive oil)
- parmesan cheese - 1/2 cup, grated

Steps:

1. Immerse the flattened chicken in a glass bowl with the pepper, milk, and salt for approximately 10 minutes.
2. Coat the air fryer basket with the cooking spray (olive oil) and heat the air fryer to the temperature of 400°F.
3. In an additional dish, blend the parmesan cheese, breadcrumbs, and Asiago cheese.
4. Transfer the chicken breasts to the breadcrumb mixture and compress the crumbs to ensure they stick.
5. Move 2 chicken breasts to the basket of the hot air fryer and apply the cooking spray to the top of the chicken. You will need to do another stage with the remaining chicken breasts.
6. Heat for 4 minutes and turn the chicken over. Spray again with the cooking spray and continue to fry for another 4 minutes.
7. Remove to a plate and repeat steps 16 and 17 for the other 2 chicken breasts.
8. When you have removed the last two breasts, replace the

original 2 chicken breasts into the fryer for approximately 60 seconds to warm them.

9. Enjoy immediately.

Helpful Tip:

- You can use a combination of any type of any hard cheese that has been grated such as Romano cheese. You will need 1 cup of the combination of cheese(s).

Coconut Shrimp

Total Prep & Cooking Time: 25 minutes
Makes: 4 Helpings
Protein: 13 gm.
Net Carbs: 16 gm.
Fat: 6 gm.
Sugar: 7 gm.
Calories: 191

What you need:

- cornstarch - 1/4 cup
- two large egg whites
- salt - 1 tsp.
- large raw shrimp - 1/2 lb.
- coconut flakes - 8 oz., sweetened

Steps:

1. Blend the cornstarch and salt in a glass dish. In another dish, empty the egg whites. In a final dish, pour the coconut.
2. Use a fork to dredge the shrimp, firstly in the cornstarch, secondly the egg and finally the coconut.
3. Transfer the coated shrimp to the air fryer basket.
4. Repeat steps 2 and 3 until the basket has a layer of shrimp with room in between each. You may need to do the shrimp in stages.
5. Warm for 15 minutes at a temperature of 330°F and remove to enjoy hot.

Helpful Tips:
- You can use frozen shrimp in this recipe. Make sure that they are still cold but defrosted.

Crab Cakes

Total Prep & Cooking Time: 1 hour 20 minutes
Makes: 6 Cakes
Protein: 8 gm.
Net Carbs: 5 gm.
Fat: 5 gm.
Sugar: 1 gm.
Calories: 100

What you need:

- two eggs, large
- Dijon mustard - 1 tsp.
- Worcestershire sauce - 2 tsp.
- red bell pepper - 1/4 cup, diced finely
- old bay seasoning - 1 tsp.
- pepper - 1/4 tsp.
- green onions - two, chopped
- panko bread crumbs - 1/3 cup
- parsley - 2 tbsp., chopped finely
- lump crab meat - 16 oz.
- mayonnaise - 2 tbsp.

Steps:

1. Chop the onions and bell pepper and set to the side. Finely mince the parsley and set aside as well.
2. Using a glass bowl, whip the eggs and blend the Worcestershire sauce, pepper, mayonnaise, mustard, and old bay seasoning until well-integrated.
3. Combine the chopped vegetables, breadcrumbs and parsley to the mixture until incorporated.
4. Finally, use a rubber scraper to combine the crab meat to the mixture and do not over mix.
5. Equally, divide the batter into 6 sections and create individual patties by hand.
6. Transfer to a plate and put a piece of plastic wrap on top.
7. Refrigerate for 60 minutes and remove when ready to cook.
8. Heat for 10 minutes at a temperature of 400°F.
9. Remove and enjoy immediately.

Fried Catfish

Total Prep & Cooking Time: 1 hour 20 minutes
Makes: 4 Helpings
Protein: 24 gm.
Net Carbs: 6 gm.
Fat: 26 gm.
Sugar: 1 gm.
Calories: 208

What you need:

- 4 catfish fillets
- cooking spray (olive oil)
- 2 oz. seasoned fish fry or seafood breading mix
- 1 tbsp. parsley, chopped

Steps:

1. Adjust the temperature of the air fryer to 400°F to heat.
2. Wash the catfish and use paper towels to remove the excess moisture.
3. Empty the seasoned breading mix into a ziplock bag and transfer one fish to the bag.
4. Agitate until the fish is completely covered, shake off the excess and transfer it to a plate. Repeat step 3 for the other pieces of catfish.
5. Transfer to the hot air fryer basket and coat with the cooking spray (olive oil). You will need to fry these in stages most likely according to the size of the catfish.
6. Fry for a total of 22 minutes, carefully turning the fish over at the halfway mark.
7. Remove the fish to a clean serving dish. Repeat steps 17 through 19 until all fish are completed.
8. Garnish with the chopped parsley before serving hot.

Helpful Tip:
- If you have a larger catfish, you will need to cook them in batches, perhaps even one at a time depending on the size of your air fryer.
- Feel free to add more seasoned breading mix to the bag as the fish will need to be completely covered. If you have a

bigger fish, you will naturally need more breading.
- If you like less crispy breading, diminish the cooking time by 2 minutes.

Herbed Turkey Breast

Total Prep & Cooking Time: 45 minutes
Makes: 4 Helpings
Protein: 32 gm.
Net Carbs: 3 gm.
Fat: 10 gm.
Sugar: 1 gm.
Calories: 226

What you need:

- mustard powder - 1 tsp.
- bone-in turkey breast - 20 oz.
- garlic - 3 tsp., minced
- rosemary seasoning - 1/2 tbsp.
- pepper - 3 tsp.
- olive oil - 2 tsp.
- lemon juice - 3 tsp.
- paprika seasoning - 1/8 tsp.
- salt - 1 tbsp.
- thyme seasoning- 1/2 tbsp.

Steps:

1. Heat the air fryer to the temperature of 350°F.
2. Whisk together the rosemary, mustard powder, salt, paprika, minced garlic, thyme, and pepper.
3. Combine the olive oil and lemon juice to the seasonings and integrate completely.
4. Use a pastry brush to apply the seasonings to the turkey breast.
5. Transfer to the hot basket of the air fryer with the side with the skin facing down.
6. Fry for half an hour and turn the turkey over. Continue to steam for another 20 minutes.
7. Check with a meat thermometer to ensure the turkey is at 165°F before removing from the air fryer.
8. Serve immediately and enjoy.

Pork Chops

Total Prep & Cooking Time: 15 minutes
Makes: 4 Pork Chops
Protein: 24 grams
Net Carbs: 6 grams
Fat: 26 grams
Sugar: 1 gram
Calories: 192

What you need:

- 1 tsp. paprika
- 45oz. bone-in pork chops
- 1 tsp. onion powder
- 2tbsp. avocado oil
- 1 tsp. garlic powder
- cooking spray (olive oil)
- 1tsp. salt
- 2 cloves garlic, minced

Steps:

1. Heat the air fryer to the temperature of 350°F. Coat the basket with cooking spray.
2. Blend the onion powder, 1 teaspoon of the salt, paprika and garlic powder with a whisk.
3. Combine the avocado oil and minced garlic to the seasoning and apply with a pastry brush to the top and bottom of each of the pork chops.
4. Transfer the pork chops to the hot basket of the air fryer and fry for 5 minutes.
5. Flip the pork chops to the other side. Steam for another 5 minutes.
6. Remove and enjoy immediately.

Ribeye Steak

Total Prep & Cooking Time: 35 minutes
Makes: 2 Steaks
Protein: 7 gm.
Net Carbs: 0 gm.
Fat: 4 gm.
Sugar: 2 gm.
Calories: 376

What you need:

- 2 8 oz. ribeye steak
- pepper - 1/4 tsp.
- garlic - 2 tsp., minced
- olive oil - 1 tbsp.
- salt - 3/4 tsp.
- parsley - 2 tbsp., chopped
- cooking spray (olive oil)

Steps:

1. Whisk the pepper, parsley, olive oil, minced garlic, and salt until combined.
2. Apply to the entire ribeye steaks using a pastry brush and set aside for 15 minutes.
3. Apply the cooking spray to the basket of the air fryer and heat to the temperature of 400°F.
4. Transfer the prepped steaks to the basket, fry for 7 minutes, and then turn the steaks to the other side.
5. Fry for another 7 minutes and remove to a serving platter.
6. Check the internal temperature by using a thermometer and cooking to the desired temperature as seen below in the Helpful Tips.
7. Wait about 5 minutes before serving.

Helpful Tips:
- The cook time for the recipe is for a medium well steak. Diminish the time by 4 total minutes for medium rare and by 2 minutes if you prefer a medium steak.
- The temperatures for the level of cooked steak are as follows:
  - 125°F - rare
  - 135°F - medium rare
  - 145°F - medium
  - 150°F - medium well

Roast Beef

Total Prep & Cooking Time: 55 minutes
Makes: 6 Helpings
Protein: 25 gm.
Net Carbs: 0 gm.
Fat: 6 gm.
Sugar: 0 gm.
Calories: 320

What you need:

- salt - 1 tsp.
- beef roast - 2 lb.
- olive oil - 1 tbsp.
- rosemary seasoning - 1 tsp.

Steps:

1. Heat the air fryer to the temperature of 360°F.
2. Blend the rosemary, salt and olive oil on a plate.
3. Lay the beef into the seasoning and flip over to the other side to cover the meat fully.
4. Transfer the beef to the basket of the air fryer and steam for a total of 45 minutes.
5. Remove from the air fryer to a platter. Layer tin foil over the meat for about 10 minutes.
6. Take the tin foil off and serve while hot.

Rotisserie Chicken

Total Prep & Cooking Time: 1 hour 20 minutes
Makes: 4 Helpings
Protein: 22 gm.
Net Carbs: 2 gm.
Fat: 11 gm.
Sugar: 1 gm.
Calories: 296

What you need:

- pepper - 1/4 tsp.
- 1 whole chicken, approximately 4 lbs.
- red pepper flakes - 1/4 tsp.
- butter - 2 tbsp.
- salt - 3/4 tsp., separated
- thyme seasoning - 1/4 tsp.

Steps:

1. Clean the chicken by removing the insides and remove the moisture by using several paper towels.
2. Blend the pepper, butter, red pepper flakes, 1/4 teaspoon of the salt and thyme in a small dish until totally combined.
3. Spoon the seasoned mixture in the middle of the meat and skin of the chicken on both sides of the breasts.
4. Apply pressure with your fingers to move the seasonings throughout the breasts.
5. Sprinkle the remaining 1/2 teaspoon of salt over the entire chicken.
6. Insert the wire basket inside your air fryer and transfer the entire chicken inside with the breast side down.
7. Heat for half an hour at a temperature of 365°F.
8. Carefully flip the chicken over using tongs and continue to cook for an additional half hour.
9. Remove the juicy roasted chicken to a plate and wait approximately ten minutes before slicing and serving.

Salmon Fillets

Total Prep & Cooking Time: 45 minutes
Makes: 2 Fillets
Protein: 22 gm.
Net Carbs: 0 gm.
Fat: 7 gm.
Sugar: 2 gm.
Calories: 150

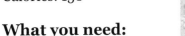

What you need:

- garlic - 2 cloves, minced
- rice wine vinegar - 3 tbsp.
- orange zest - 2 tsp., grated finely
- orange juice - 1/2 cup
- salmon fillets - 2 5 oz.
- soy sauce - 1/4 cup
- olive oil - 3 tsp.
- salt - 1/2 tsp.
- ginger - 1 tbsp., minced

Steps:

1. Fully blend the ginger, orange zest, soy sauce, garlic, vinegar, orange juice, salt and olive oil in a glass dish.
2. Split the mixture in half and spoon half into a ziplock bag.
3. Transfer the salmon fillets to the ziplock bag and seal the bag.
4. Place the ziplock bag on the counter to marinate for half an hour.
5. After the time has lapsed, drain the salmon fillets extremely well.
6. Arrange the drained fillets in the basket of the air fryer and heat for 12 minutes at a temperature of 400°F.
7. Remove the salmon to a serving plate and empty the remaining marinade liquid over the plate.
8. Serve immediately and enjoy!

Shrimp Scampi

Total Prep & Cooking Time: 20 minutes
Makes: 4 Helpings
Protein: 16 gm.
Net Carbs: 2.3 gm.
Fat: 13 gm.
Sugar: 0 gm.
Calories: 191

What you need:

- lemon juice - 1 tbsp.
- shrimp - 16 oz., peeled and deveined
- garlic - 1 tbsp., minced
- red pepper flakes 2 tsp.
- chives seasoning - 1 tbsp.
- butter - 4 tbsp., salted
- basil - 2 tbsp., chopped
- basil seasoning - 1 tsp.
- chicken broth - 2 tbsp.

Steps:

1. Install a 7-inch baking pan into the air fryer basket. Adjust the temperature of the air fryer to 325°F for approximately 8 minutes.
2. While the air fryer is heating up, combine the red pepper flakes, garlic, lemon juice, and cold butter in a dish.
3. Once warmed, remove the baking pan with oven mitts and empty the contents of the bowl into the pan. Replace the pan into the basket and fry for 2 minutes at the same temperature.
4. Remove the hot pan and insert the chopped basil, chicken broth, chives, and shrimp. Blend to cover the shrimp completely in the liquid and seasonings.
5. Transfer the pan back to the air fryer basket and heat for another 5 minutes and gently shaking at the halfway mark.
6. Remove the pan to a wire rack for about 60 seconds after turning the shrimp to ensure they are totally covered in the sauce.
7. Distribute to serving dishes and garnish with the basil seasoning before serving.

Tilapia Fillets

Total Prep & Cooking Time: 10 minutes
Makes: 2 helpings
Protein: 23 gm.
Net Carbs: 0 gm.
Fat: 2 gm.
Sugar: 0 gm.
Calories: 112

What you need:

- cooking spray (olive oil)
- 2 tilapia fillets
- lemon pepper - 1/2 tsp.
- butter - 3 tsp.
- salt - 1/4 tsp.
- old bay seasoning - 1/2 tsp.

Steps:

1. Combine the salt, old bay seasoning, butter, and lemon pepper until blended.
2. Apply the seasonings to the top and bottom of the tilapia fillets with a pastry brush.
3. Coat the inside of the basket in the air fryer and transfer the fillets to the basket in a single layer.
4. Spray the fillets with the olive oil and warm at a temperature of 400°F for 7 minutes.
5. Before removing to a serving platter, make sure the fish is completely cooked by flaking easily with a fork.
6. Serve immediately and enjoy!

Chapter 7: International Recipes

Carne Asada Mexican Taco Plate

Total Prep & Cooking Time: 35 minutes plus 3 hours to marinate
Makes: 4 Helpings
Protein: 23 gm.
Net Carbs: 2 gm.
Fat: 11 gm.
Sugar: 0 gm.
Calories: 190

What you need:

For the meat:
- 1 large yellow onion, sliced thinly
- 2 lbs. skirt steak, approximately ½-inch thick

For the marinade:
- lemon juice - 1/4 cup
- olive oil - 2 tbsp.
- 5 whole chipotle peppers in adobo
- lime juice - 1/4 cup
- 2 pasilla peppers
- orange juice - 1/2 cup
- ground cumin seasoning - 2 tsp.
- cilantro leaves - 1 cup
- brown sugar - 2 tbsp.
- salt - 3 tsp., separated
- garlic - 1 clove, crushed
- oregano seasoning - 2 tsp.
- pepper - 1 tsp.

Steps:

1. Place the pasilla peppers over medium heat over your stove burner and turn with tongs until they turn black.
2. Turn the burner off and move the peppers to a paper towel to cool.

3. After approximately 5 minutes, use rubber gloves to remove the skins and set to the side.
4. Using a food blender, whisk the crushed garlic, ground cumin, cilantro leaves, salt, brown sugar, oregano, and pepper for about 10 seconds.
5. Combine the lemon juice, chipotle peppers, lime juice, charred pasilla peppers, orange juice and olive oil in the blender and pulse for an additional 30 seconds until fully incorporated.
6. Separate 1/2 cup of the marinade and empty into a separate dish.
7. In a lidded tub, transfer the remaining marinade and immerse the onions and skirt steak in the juice completely.
8. Refrigerate for 3 hours at least or overnight.
9. When the meat is properly marinated, heat the air fryer to the temperature of 400°F.
10. Remove the marinated meat from the fridge and thoroughly drain.
11. Transfer to the air fryer basket in one layer and steam for approximately 10 minutes, shaking the basket at the 5-minute mark.
12. Remove the onions and meat from the basket and set on a plate for about 5 minutes.
13. Cut the steak into thin slices against the grain and cover the dish with the remaining marinade.
14. Serve with your favorite taco toppings.

Helpful tip:
- You can substitute jalapeno or poblano peppers in place of the pasilla peppers if you cannot find them.

Crab Rangoon

Total Prep & Cooking Time: 20 minutes
Makes: 4 Helpings, 4 pieces per Helping
Protein: 8 gm.
Net Carbs: 4 gm.
Fat: 4 gm.
Sugar: 6 gm.
Calories: 164

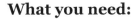

What you need:

- 3 1/2 tbsp. green onions, diced
- 1/2 tsp. Worcestershire sauce
- 4 oz. crab meat, finely diced
- salt - 1/8 tsp.
- 3 1/2 oz. cream cheese, softened
- 16 wonton wrappers
- 1/2 tbsp. olive oil
- Water

Steps:

1. Use a rubber spatula to cream the Worcestershire sauce, diced green onions, cream cheese, salt, and crab meat until incorporated fully.
2. Fill a small dish with water and keep handy.
3. Spoon the filling into the 16 individual wonton wrappers.
4. Dip your fingers into the water dish and run it on the edges of a wonton wrapper to wet them. Press the opposing edges together firmly on one side and then the other to finish with the pinched section on the top of the wrapper.
5. Repeat step 4 for all the wontons.
6. Apply the olive oil to the total wonton with a pastry brush.
7. Arrange the wontons in a single layer and allowing room to in between. You will most likely need to do these in stages.
8. Heat at a temperature of 360°F for approximately 6 minutes and remove to a serving plate.
9. Repeat steps 6 and 7 until all the wontons are complete.
10. Enjoy immediately.

Helpful Tip:
- You can substitute 8 egg roll wrappers for the wonton wrappers. Just cut them in half to be the correct size.

Egg Rolls

Total Prep & Cooking Time: 45 minutes
Makes: 4 Helpings
Protein: 4 gm.
Net Carbs: 28 gm.
Fat: 5 gm.
Sugar: 4 gm.
Calories: 190

What you need:

- 4 tbsp. olive oil, separated
- 3 cups green cabbage, shredded
- 1 clove garlic, grated
- 4 oz. red cabbage, shredded
- 1 tsp. ginger, grated
- 4 oz. carrots, shredded
- 1 scallion, sliced thinly
- 3 tsp. lime juice
- 1/2 cup onions, diced
- 10 oz. medium shrimp
- 2 tsp. soy sauce
- 1 large egg white
- 8 egg roll wrappers
- 2 tbsp. water

Steps:

1. Cover a flat sheet with baking lining and set to the side.
2. Warm 2 tbsp. of olive oil in a non-stick skillet and heat the shrimp while occasionally stirring until they turn pink throughout which should take about 2 minutes.
3. Remove the shrimp to a plate using a slotted spoon and let them rest for approximately 5 minutes.
4. Separate 8 whole shrimp and keep to the side. Chop the remaining shrimp into small sections.
5. Warm the remaining 2 tablespoons of olive oil for about 30 seconds using the same skillet.
6. Toss the diced onions and fry for approximately 3 minutes while occasionally stirring.

7. Then empty the ginger and garlic into the skillet and heat for an additional 60 seconds.
8. Combine the scallion, red and green cabbage, water and carrots into the skillet. Sauté for approximately 3 minutes and remove the skillet from the burner.
9. Blend the soy sauce, lime juice, and diced shrimp into the vegetable mixture until integrated fully.
10. Heat the air fryer to the temperature of 375°F.
11. In a small dish, whip the egg white and use the prepped sheet to place the egg rolls wrappers side by side.
12. Use a pastry brush to apply the egg to the edges of the wrappers.
13. Spoon about 1/2 cup of the vegetable mixture on the center base portion of the wrapper. Leave space on the edges where there is no filling.
14. Top with a whole shrimp and rotate the wrapper away from you while tucking in the sides to encase the filling fully.
15. Repeat for the other 7 egg rolls.
16. Completely cover the egg rolls with olive oil and transfer to the basket of the air fryer.
17. Fry for a total of 7 minutes while rolling them over halfway through the cook time.
18. Remove and enjoy while hot.

General Tso's Chicken

Total Prep & Cooking Time: 30 minutes
Makes: 4 Helpings
Protein: 9 gm.
Net Carbs: 23 gm.
Fat: 5 gm.
Sugar: 2 gm.
Calories: 430

What you need:

- brown sugar - 3/4 cup
- chicken thighs - 2 lbs., boneless and skinless
- potato starch - 1/3 cup
- 3 green onions, chopped
- sesame oil - 1 tsp.
- garlic - 2 tsp., minced
- ginger - 1 tsp., minced
- chicken broth - 4 oz.
- rice vinegar - 2 tbsp.
- olive oil - 1 tbsp.
- corn starch - 2 tsp.
- cold water - 1/4 cup
- soy sauce - 4 oz.
- 2 dried red chilies
- cooking spray (olive oil)
- salt - 1/4 tsp.

Steps:

1. Heat the air fryer to the temperature of 400°F. Apply a coat of cooking spray on the inside of the air fryer basket.
2. Chop the meat into small chunks and toss in a glass dish with the potato starch to cover completely.
3. Transfer to the basket of the air fryer using tongs and steam for a total of approximately 25 minutes. Make sure to toss the basket about every 5 minutes to ensure they are properly cooked.
4. In the meantime, use a skillet to warm the olive oil for approximately 30 seconds.

123

5. Combine the garlic, dried chilies, ginger, and green onions in the skillet for about 60 seconds.
6. Then blend the chicken broth, rice vinegar, brown sugar, salt, and sesame oil into the hot skillet. Turn the heat up to simmer and occasionally blend for an additional 3 minutes while the mixture reduces.
7. Remove the chicken from the air fryer basket and transfer to the skillet. Stir to combine well.
8. Blend in the cold water and the cornstarch and stir for about 60 seconds while the sauce thickens.
9. Remove to a serving plate and enjoy!

Indian Paneer Pappad

Total Prep & Cooking Time: 20 minutes
Makes: 4 Helpings
Protein: 2 gm.
Net Carbs: 7 gm.
Fat: 0 gm.
Sugar: 0 gm.
Calories: 41

What you need:

- 1/4 tsp. garam masala
- 10 oz. paneer, thick and long slices
- 1/2 tsp. red chili powder
- 5 pappads, roasted
- 1/4 cup water
- 4 oz. all-purpose flour
- cooking spray (olive oil)

Steps:

1. Combine the chili powder, garam masala and paneer in a glass dish making sure the cheese is covered in the seasonings fully.
2. In a separate dish, blend the water and flour and on a plate, crush the pappads into small pieces.
3. Coat each slice of paneer in the flour and then roll in the pappad crumbs, completely covering the paneer.
4. Apply the olive oil spray to the top of the paneer sticks and transfer into the basket of the air fryer making sure there is room in between each piece.
5. Adjust the air fryer temperature to 360°F and heat for approximately 4 minutes.
6. Flip the paneer over to the other side and spray once again with the olive oil. Steam for another 3 minutes.
7. Serve immediately and enjoy while hot.

Indian Samosas

Total Prep & Cooking Time: 70 minutes
Makes: 5 Helpings, 2 Samosas per Helping
Protein: 6 gm.
Net Carbs: 12 gm.
Fat: 7 gm.
Sugar: 1 gm.
Calories: 84

What you need:

For the samosa breading:
- all-purpose flour - 1 1/2 cups
- salt - 1/2 tsp.
- thyme seasoning - 1 tsp.
- water - 2/3 cup
- olive oil - 4 tbsp., separated

For the filling:
- turmeric powder - 1/2 tsp.
- coriander powder - 1 tsp.
- ginger - 1/2 tsp., minced
- 3 russet potatoes
- garlic - 1/2 tsp., minced
- 2 green chilies, chopped
- green peas - 1/3 cup
- mustard seeds - 1/2 tsp.
- 4 curry leaves
- salt - 1 1/2 tsp., separated
- 1 large onion
- chili powder - 3/4 tsp.
- cumin powder - 1/2 tsp.
- lemon juice - 3 tbsp.
- sesame seeds - 1 tsp.
- olive oil - 3 tbsp., separated
- garam masala - 1/2 tsp.
- water - 6 cups
- coriander - 2 tbsp., chopped

126

Steps:

1. Peel the skins off the potatoes by using a vegetable peeler.
2. Warm the 6 cups of water in a saucepan with one teaspoon of the salt and bring to a simmer.
3. Lower the setting to medium, transfer the skinned potatoes to the pot and cover with a lid.
4. Bake the russet potatoes for approximately 15 minutes until they are tender and remove from the stove.
5. Thoroughly drain the water and crush the potatoes completely with a masher. Set to the side.
6. Dissolve 2 tbsps. of olive oil in a hot wok and toss in the curry leaves and mustard seeds.
7. After about half a minute, blend the ginger, chopped onions, and garlic before frying for approximately 2 minutes.
8. Combine the peas, green chilies, 1/2 teaspoon of the salt and chopped coriander and incorporate fully for about 30 seconds.
9. Blend the turmeric, chili powder, coriander powder, lemon juice, garam masala in the wok and sauté for an additional 2 minutes.
10. Fully incorporate the mashed potatoes in the wok, blending fully for another 3 minutes. Remove the filling from the burner.
11. In a food blender, whip the olive oil, salt, thyme and 1/2 cup of the water for approximately 2 minutes. The consistency will become thick dough.
12. Cover a dishcloth on top of the bowl and let it sit for 15 minutes.
13. Set a shallow dish out with the remaining 1/8 cup of water.
14. Section the dough in 10 equal sections. Flatten each section into rectangles about six inches wide and four inches tall with a rolling pin.
15. Heat the air fryer to the temperature of 360°F.
16. Slice the dough in diagonals to create 2 triangles. Spoon approximately 1 tablespoon of filling into one triangle and cover with the other triangle.
17. Dip your fingers in the dish of water and run on the edges of the dough.
18. Compress and crimp along the entire edge.
19. Repeat steps 15 through 17 for each of the samosas.
20. Use a pastry brush to completely cover the samosas in the

last 2 tablespoons of oil and dust the tops with the sesame seeds.

21. Insert the samosas into the basket of the air fryer and steam for approximately 17 minutes.

22. Remove to a serving plate and enjoy immediately.

Mexican Churros

Total Prep & Cooking Time: 10 minutes
Makes: 8 Churros
Protein: 4 gm.
Net Carbs: 16 gm.
Fat: 3 gm.
Sugar: 6 gm.
Calories: 102

What you need:

- 1/2 cup all-purpose flour
- 1 8 oz. can refrigerated crescent rolls
- 2 tbsp. butter
- 1 tbsp. ground cinnamon
- 2 tbsp. sugar, granulated

Steps:

1. Use baking lining to cover a flat sheet and set to the side.
2. Dissolve the butter in a pot and take away from the burner. Set aside.
3. Heat the air fryer to the temperature of 330°F.
4. Blend the cinnamon and sugar in a glass dish with a whisk.
5. Evenly spread the flour on a flat surface and open the can of crescent rolls.
6. Flatten the 4 sections of rectangle dough onto the flour and compress the perforations in the dough to make one uniform piece.
7. Coat the melted butter onto the flattened dough.
8. Dust two of the pieces of dough with a tablespoon each of with the sugar mixture covering to the edges.
9. Place the additional pieces of dough on top of the sugar mixture with the buttered dough on the top and slightly press the edges.
10. Cut each section of dough into 4 equal strips with a knife or pizza cutter.
11. Rotate each strip of dough to create a twist and transfer to the hot basket of the air fryer in a single layer.
12. Broil for approximately 5 minutes and remove to the prepped flat sheet.

13. Apply the butter to the top of the churros and dust with a tablespoon of the sugar mixture.
14. Turn the churros over and apply the remaining butter and the last tablespoon of the sugar mixture, completely covering the churros.
15. Serve immediately and enjoy!

Mexican Corn on the Cob

Total Prep & Cooking Time: 20 minutes
Makes: 4 Cobs
Protein: 4 gm.
Net Carbs: 16 gm.
Fat: 3 gm.
Sugar: 6 gm.
Calories: 102

What you need:

- 1/4 tsp. pepper
- 4 pieces corn on the cob
- 1/8 tsp. salt
- 2 oz. feta cheese
- 1/8 tsp. onion powder
- 1/4 tsp. chili powder

Steps:

1. Shell the corn and clean thoroughly. Insert into the air fryer basket and heat for 10 minutes at a temperature of 390°F.
2. Open the lid and dust the corn with the feta cheese. Continue to fry for another 5 minutes.
3. Distribute the corn to a plate and dust with the chili powder, salt, onion powder, and pepper.
4. Serve immediately and enjoy!

Spicy Chicken Wontons

Total Prep & Cooking Time: 20 minutes
Makes: 6 Helpings
Protein: 9 gm.
Net Carbs: 10 gm.
Fat: 15 gm.
Sugar: 1 gm.
Calories: 192

What you need:

- 1 cup chicken, shredded
- 1 tbsp. buffalo sauce
- 1 scallion, green, sliced thinly
- 2 tbsp. blue cheese, crumbled
- 12 wonton wrappers
- 1/8 cup water
- cooking spray (olive oil)
- 8 oz. cream cheese, softened

Steps:

1. Cover the shredded chicken with the buffalo sauce in a glass dish and set to the side.
2. Using a food blender, pulse the cream cheese, spiced chicken, scallion and blue cheese for approximately 60 seconds until combined.
3. Heat the air fryer to the temperature of 400°F.
4. Empty the water into a shallow dish.
5. Lay the wonton wrappers side by side on the counter or baking sheet.
6. Spoon about a tablespoon of the filling into each wrapper.
7. Wet the edges of one wonton wrapper after you have dipped your fingers with the water.
8. Crimp the opposing corners of the wrapper and then press the other opposing sides together to enclose the filling fully.
9. Repeat steps 7 and 8 until all wontons are crimped.
10. Grease the basket with the cooking spray in addition to the base of each wonton.
11. Arrange the wontons in the basket without touching each other.

12. Heat for approximately 4 minutes and remove to a serving plate.
13. Repeat steps 11 and 12 if it is necessary to fry in stages.
14. Enjoy immediately.

Helpful Tip:
- You can create the filling and refrigerate ahead of time. The mixture will keep for 7 days or will work as a dip at your next party.

Sweet & Sour Tofu and Broccoli Meal

Total Prep & Cooking Time: 30 minutes
Makes: 5 Helpings
Protein: 4 gm.
Net Carbs: 16 gm.
Fat: 3 gm.
Sugar: 6 gm.
Calories: 102

What you need:

- maple syrup - 2 tbsp.
- tofu - 16oz., extra firm
- 1 clove garlic, minced
- soy sauce - 2 tbsp.
- ginger - 1 tsp., minced
- sriracha - 4 tbsp.

Steps:

1. Adjust the temperature of the air fryer to 400°F.
2. Drain the tofu and slice into cubes about half an inch wide.
3. Transfer to the basket of the air fryer and heat for approximately 15 minutes.
4. Be sure to agitate the basket about every 5 minutes.
5. Meanwhile, blend the minced garlic, maple syrup, minced ginger, soy sauce and sriracha in a glass dish until fully incorporated.
6. Remove the tofu from the air fryer to a dish, drizzle the sauce to cover the tofu by tossing completely.
7. Serve with steamed broccoli or rice and enjoy!

Tempeh Sandwich

Total Prep & Cooking Time: 1 hour
Makes: 2 Sandwiches
Protein: 11 gm.
Net Carbs: 14 gm.
Fat: 4 gm.
Sugar: 4 gm.
Calories: 182

What you need:

- soy sauce - 2 tbsp.
- garlic powder - 1/2 tsp.
- tempeh - 8 oz.
- 4 slices whole grain bread
- 4 tomato slices
- 4 lettuce leaves
- liquid smoke - 1/2 tsp.
- rice vinegar - 1 tbsp.
- ketchup - 3 tsp.
- 1 avocado
- paprika seasoning - 1/2 tsp.

Steps:

1. Combine the rice vinegar, garlic powder, liquid smoke, soy sauce, ketchup and paprika in a zip lock bag. Seal tightly and shake to blend fully.
2. Cut the tempeh into thin strips and transfer to the ziplock bag.
3. Set the ziplock bag on the counter for at least 30 minutes to marinate or better overnight.
4. After the marinating is complete, drain the tempeh thoroughly and reserve the marinade for later.
5. Lay the tempeh in the basket of the air fryer and heat for approximately 14 minutes at a temperature of 325°F.
6. In the meantime, prepare the bread in the toaster if you wish and apply your favorite condiments.
7. Cut the avocado into wedges or mash if you prefer.
8. Remove the tempeh to one slice of the bread and drizzle the

remaining marinade over the top.
9. Layer the tomatoes, lettuce, and avocado on top of the tempeh and finish with the last slice of bread.
10. Serve immediately and enjoy!

Chapter 8: Sweet Treat and Dessert Recipes

Apple Cake

Total Prep & Cooking Time: 25 minutes
Makes: 2 Helpings
Protein: 24 gm.
Net Carbs: 6 gm.
Fat: 26 gm.
Sugar: 1 gm.
Calories: 310

What you need:

- apple - 2 cups, diced finely
- all-purpose flour - 5 tbsp.
- sugar - 2 tbsp., granulated
- ground cinnamon - 1/2 tsp.
- butter - 2 tbsp.

Steps:

1. Heat the air fryer to the temperature of 350°F.
2. Use a ramekin or baking pan to empty 2 cups of the diced apple.
3. In another dish, blend the sugar, cinnamon, flour, and butter until thoroughly combined.
4. Dust the top of the apples with the dry mixture and transfer the pan to the air fryer basket.
5. Fry for 15 minutes and remove to the counter.
6. Wait approximately 5 minutes before serving and enjoy!

Apple Dumplings

Total Prep & Cooking Time: 40 minutes
Makes: 4 Helpings
Protein: 24 gm.
Net Carbs: 6 gm.
Fat: 26 gm.
Sugar: 1 gm.
Calories: 192

What you need:

- 4 small apples
- 4 tbsp. raisins
- 2 tbsp. brown sugar
- 4 sheets puff pastry
- 4 tbsp. butter

Steps:

1. Prepare a flat sheet covered with baking lining and set to the side.
2. Liquefy the butter in a hot pot and take away from the burner. Set aside.
3. Set the puff pastry sheets side by side on the prepped flat sheet.
4. Use a paring knife to peel the apples and then core. Transfer each apple to the middle of a puff pastry.
5. Heat the air fryer to the temperature of 360°F and line the basket with a layer of tin foil.
6. In a glass dish, integrate the brown sugar and raisins. Divide the mixture equally between the apples and pour into the core of each.
7. Enclose the apple fully with the puff pastry by folding around the apple.
8. Apply the cooled butter over the entire dumpling with a pastry brush and transfer to the hot air fryer with the folded edge down.
9. Fry the dumplings for a total of 25 minutes while flipping them over halfway through.
10. Remove to a serving dish and wait for approximately 10 minutes before serving.

Blackberry Cobbler

Total Prep & Cooking Time: 25 minutes
Makes: 1 personal Cobbler
Protein: 3 gm.
Net Carbs: 22 gm.
Fat: 10 gm.
Sugar: 5 gm.
Calories: 200

What you need:

- 4 tbsp. butter
- 2 cups blackberries
- 1 cup all-purpose flour
- 1/2 tsp. vanilla extract
- 1 large egg
- 1/2 cup sugar, granulated
- 1 tsp. sugar, granulated and separate

Steps:

1. Dissolve the butter in a pot and take away from the burner. Set to the side.
2. Heat the air fryer to the temperature of 350°F.
3. Use a 5-inch baking pan to empty the blackberries. Dust with 1/2 teaspoon of the sugar.
4. In a separate dish, blend the melted butter, vanilla extract, egg, flour and 1/2 cup of the sugar until fully together.
5. Spoon the batter on top of the blackberries and flatten with a rubber scraper or spoon to even the crust across the top of the whole pan.
6. Use a knife to puncture the crust in several areas and dust the top of the crust with the remaining 1/2 teaspoon of sugar.
7. Layer a piece of tin foil over the entire dish including the bottom. Slice a hole into the top of the foil and transfer to the hot air fryer basket.
8. Steam for 10 minutes and remove to the counter.
9. Take the tin foil off and serve immediately while hot.

Bread and Butter Pudding

Total Prep & Cooking Time: 35 minutes
Makes: 2 Helpings
Protein: 0 gm.
Net Carbs: 10 gm.
Fat: 0 gm.
Sugar: 6 gm.
Calories: 64

What you need:

- cooking spray (olive oil)
- sugar - 1 1/2 tsp., granulated
- 5 oz. milk
- one egg, preferably large
- butter - 3 tsp.
- raisins - 1/2 cup
- 1/2 cup almonds, sliced
- white bread - 3 slices
- ground cinnamon - 1/2 tbsp.

Steps:

1. Apply a coat of the cooking spray (olive oil) to a 5-inch baking pan.
2. In a glass dish, blend the cinnamon and sugar together.
3. Remove the crust from the slices of bread and spread the butter over each slice.
4. Heat the air fryer to the temperature of 320°F.
5. Dust each piece of bread with the sugar blend and transfer to the baking pan.
6. In a separate dish, whip the egg and empty into the pan along 1/4 cup of raisins and 1/4 cup of the sliced almonds.
7. Move the pan into the basket of the hot air fryer and steam for approximately 25 minutes.
8. Remove and serve immediately while hot.

Cheesecake Rolls

Total Prep & Cooking Time: 35 minutes
Makes: 6 Rolls
Protein: 5 gm.
Net Carbs: 18 gm.
Fat: 6 gm.
Sugar: 5 gm.
Calories: 130

What you need:

- sugar - 1/4 cup, granulated
- cream cheese - 6 oz., softened
- butter - 3/4 tbsp., unsalted
- vanilla extract - 1 tsp.
- cooking spray (olive oil)
- fig jam - 1/3 cup
- water - 3 tsp.
- one large egg
- 6 egg roll wrappers
- lemon juice - 1 tsp.
- sugar - 1/8 cup, granulated and separate
- ground cinnamon - 1/3 tsp.

Steps:

1. Use a hot pot to dissolve the butter and take away from the burner. Set to the side.
2. In the meantime, cover a flat sheet with baking paper and line the egg roll wrappers side by side with the corners facing the bottom.
3. Whip the egg and combine with the water thoroughly in a glass dish. Set to the side.
4. Using a food blender, pulse the lemon juice, vanilla extract, cream cheese and the 1/4 cup of sugar for about 2 minutes until smooth.
5. Spoon the filling into a pastry bag.
6. Squeeze approximately 2 tablespoons of the filling onto the middle of the wrapper. Repeat for each roll.
7. Scoop a tablespoon of the fig jam on top of the filling of each wrapper.

141

8. Using a pastry brush, coat the edges of the egg wrappers with the egg wash.
9. Rotate the bottom edge over the filling and crimp in the edges as you rotate.
10. Apply additional egg wash to the top corner to fully seal the egg roll.
11. Repeat steps 8 through 10 for the other egg rolls.
12. Coat the egg rolls all over with the olive oil.
13. Place a piece of tin foil on the base of the air fryer basket and move the prepared egg rolls inside the basket.
14. Heat for approximately 6 minutes.
15. Meanwhile, blend the cinnamon and sugar in a glass dish.
16. Remove the egg rolls to a serving platter and apply the melted butter with a pastry brush.
17. Dust the sugar mixture over the top of each egg rolls and serve immediately.

Helpful Tip:
- You can easily create a homemade pastry bag with a large sized zip lock bag. Add the filling and slice the bottom corner with scissors.

Chocolate Chip Cookies

Total Prep & Cooking Time: 20 minutes
Makes: 12 Cookies (2 Cookies per Helping)
Protein: 2 gm.
Net Carbs: 24 gm.
Fat: 7 gm.
Sugar: 6 gm.
Calories: 170

What you need:

- baking soda - 1/4 tsp.
- salt - 1/8tsp.
- butter - 2 oz., unsalted and softened
- 1 egg yolk
- sugar - 2 tbsp., granulated
- semi-sweet chocolate chips - 4 oz.
- brown sugar - 1/3 cup
- all-purpose flour - 2/3 cup
- vanilla extract - 1/2tsp.

Steps:

1. Place a section of tin foil on the bottom of the air fryer basket and heat to the temperature of 350°F.
2. Using a food blender, pulse the baking soda, flour, and salt for about 15 seconds.
3. Combine the butter, granulated sugar, vanilla extract, egg yolk, and brown sugar for an additional 60 seconds until smooth.
4. Use a rubber scraper to blend the chocolate chips into the batter.
5. Spoon the batter using a cookie scoop and roll into mounds. Transfer to the basket of the air fryer about two inches away from each other.
6. Broil the cookies for approximately 5 minutes.
7. Repeat steps 5 and 6 as necessary.
8. Remove the cookies by lifting the tin foil out of the basket and transferring to a wire rack.
9. Wait about 10 minutes before serving.

Helpful Tip:
- This is an adaptable recipe and can add your favorite toppings to the ingredients quite easily. Consider blending pecans, walnuts, cranberries or different flavors of chips into the batter.

Chocolate Lava Cake

Total Prep & Cooking Time: 15 minutes
Makes: 1 Cake
Protein: 2 gm.
Net Carbs: 9 gm.
Fat: 8 gm.
Sugar: 5 gm.
Calories: 60

What you need:

- two eggs, large
- salt - 1/4 tsp.
- coconut oil - 1 tbsp.
- baking powder - 1/2 tbsp.
- water - 2 tbsp.
- vanilla extract - 1/4 tsp.
- honey - 2 tbsp.
- cocoa powder - 2 tbsp.

Steps:

1. Heat the air fryer to a temperature of 350°F.
2. Use a ramekin to blend the coconut oil, eggs, cocoa powder, water, salt, honey, and vanilla extract until thoroughly combined.
3. Set the ramekin inside the basket of the air fryer and fry for approximately 8 minutes.
4. Using oven mitts, remove the dish to the counter. Wait about 5 minutes before serving hot.

Cinnamon Apple Turnovers

Total Prep & Cooking Time: 30 minutes
Makes: 12 Turnovers
Protein: 3 gm.
Net Carbs: 28 gm.
Fat: 5 gm.
Sugar: 7 gm.
Calories: 164

What you need:

- 1 tsp. ground cinnamon
- 12 empanada wrappers
- 1 tsp. vanilla extract
- 2 apples, diced (red or green)
- 1/8 tsp. nutmeg seasoning
- 4 tbsp. honey
- cooking spray (olive oil)
- 2 tsp. cornstarch
- 1 tsp. water

Steps:

1. Prepare a flat sheet by layering with baking lining. Arrange the empanada wrappers on the pan side by side.
2. Use a saucepan and combine the ground cinnamon, honey, nutmeg, diced apples and vanilla extract and heat over medium for approximately 3 minutes.
3. In a glass dish, blend the water and cornstarch thoroughly. Empty into the saucepan and heat for an additional half a minute.
4. Spoon the filling into each of the empanada wrappers.
5. Rotate and compress the ends of the wrappers to enclose the filling entirely creating a half circle.
6. Transfer the prepared turnovers to the basket of the air fryer and steam for 8 minutes at a temperature of 400°F.
7. Flip the turnovers to the other side. Steam for another 10 minutes.
8. Transfer to a plate and wait about 5 minutes before serving.

Helpful Tips:
- You can layer the turnovers in the air fryer basket, but no more than 2 layers.
- Alternatively, you can use a fork to crimp the edges of the empanada wrappers to close the turnovers properly.

Cinnamon Sugar Donuts

Total Prep & Cooking Time: 20 minutes
Makes: 8 Donuts
Protein: 3 gm.
Net Carbs: 55 gm.
Fat: 9 gm.
Sugar: 29 gm.
Calories: 320

What you need:

- 16.4 oz. can refrigerated biscuits, flaky
- 1 1/2 tsps. ground cinnamon
- coconut oil cooking spray
- 1/2 cup sugar, granulated

Steps:

1. Using a saucepan, liquefy the butter and take off from the burner. Set to the side.
2. Remove the biscuit dough from the can and separate into 8 separate pieces on a cutting board or a baking lining covered flat sheet.
3. Use a 1-inch cookie cutter to remove the middle of the dough.
4. Coat the basket of the air fryer with the coconut oil cooking spray and transfer the cut dough into the basket.
5. Heat at a temperature of 350°F for approximately 6 minutes.
6. In the meantime, blend the sugar and cinnamon on either a plate or a shallow dish.
7. Remove the doughnuts and place on a platter.
8. Apply the cooled melted butter to the top of each donut with a pastry brush.
9. Turn the donuts over onto the sugar mixture plate to coat.
10. Serve immediately and enjoy!

Helpful Tip:
- You can use the extra dough to make donut holes. Roll the dough into mounds and follow steps 24 through 29. Diminish the cooking time to 4 minutes.

Fried Oreos

Total Prep & Cooking Time: 15 minutes
Makes: 2 Oreos
Protein: 3 gm.
Net Carbs: 11 gm.
Fat: 3 gm.
Sugar: 5 gm.
Calories: 192

What you need:

- 1/4 tsp. vanilla extract
- 2 Oreo cookies
- 1/4 cup self-rising flour
- 2 tsp. sugar, confectioner
- 1/4 cup Greek yogurt

Steps:

1. Blend the flour, vanilla extract and Greek yogurt in a glass dish until it thickens into a dough.
2. Flatten the dough on a flat surface using a rolling pin and divide into half.
3. Encase one Oreo into each section and pinch the dough to cover the Oreo cookie completely.
4. Move to the air fryer basket and steam for approximately 9 minutes at a temperature of 380°F.
5. Turn the Oreos over at the halfway mark and then remove to a plate.
6. Dust with the confectioner sugar and serve while hot.

Fudge Brownies

Total Prep & Cooking Time: 35 minutes
Makes: 16 Brownies (up to 16)
Protein: 2 gm.
Net Carbs: 15 gm.
Fat: 3 gm.
Sugar: 5 gm.
Calories: 80

What you need:

- cooking spray (olive oil)
- 10.25 oz. brownie mix
- 2 tbsp. olive oil
- 1/3 cup water
- 1 large egg

Steps:

1. Integrate the water, egg, brownie mix, and olive oil in a baking pan and blend until incorporated.
2. Coat the basket of the air fryer with the cooking spray (olive oil)
3. Insert the baking pan inside the air fryer basket and heat for approximately 23 minutes at a temperature of 320°F.
4. Poke a knife into the middle of the baking pan to see if it comes out clean before removing the baking pan to the counter.
5. Wait about 10 minutes before slicing and serving.

Fruity Bread Pudding

Total Prep & Cooking Time: 40 minutes
Makes: 4 Helpings
Protein: 1 gm.
Net Carbs: 20 gm.
Fat: 5 gm.
Sugar: 11 gm.
Calories: 138

What you need:

For the pudding:
- 1/4 cup sugar, granulated
- 3 oz. all-purpose flour
- 1/2 tsp. baking powder
- 2 tbsp. milk
- 2 oz. butter, softened
- 1 large egg

For the filling:
- 4 oz. can pineapple, drained
- 2 large peaches, sliced
- 4 large plums, sliced

Steps:

1. Use a food blender to whip the sugar, flour, baking powder, butter and egg for approximately 3 minutes until smooth.
2. Use a rubber scraper to incorporate the pineapple, peaches, and plums.
3. Distribute to a baking pan and insert into the air fryer basket.
4. Heat for approximately 28 minutes at a temperature of 370°F.
5. Use oven mitts to remove the pan and place on the counter.
6. Wait about 10 minutes before serving and enjoy!

Lemon Pound Cake

Total Prep & Cooking Time: 1 hour
Makes: 8 Slices
Protein: 2 gm.
Net Carbs: 37 gm.
Fat: 7 gm.
Sugar: 27 gm.
Calories: 273

What you need:

- baking powder - 1/2 tsp.
- sugar - 8 oz., granulated
- butter - 1/2 cup, softened
- sugar - 8 oz., confectioner
- all-purpose flour - 1 tbsp., separated
- all-purpose flour - 3/4 cups
- lemon juice - 4 tbs.
- lemon juice - 1/4 cup, separated
- 2 tsp. vanilla extract
- 6-cup bundt cake pan
- two large eggs
- cooking spray (olive oil)
- salt - 1/4 tsp.

Steps:

1. Coat the bundt cake pan with the olive oil, dust with the tablespoon of flour and set to the side.
2. Heat the air fryer to the temperature of 330°F.
3. Using a food blender, pulse the baking powder, salt and the remaining 3/4 cup of flour for about 15 seconds.
4. Combine the butter, eggs, vanilla extract, 1 cup of sugar and 1/4 cup of the lemon juice and blend for about 3 minutes until the consistency is smooth.
5. Distribute the cake batter into the prepped bundt cake pan.
6. Broil for approximately 40 minutes.
7. Meanwhile, use a glass dish to combine the 4 tablespoons of lemon juice, and confectioner sugar together until blended.
8. Remove the cake out of the air fryer and set on a wire rack.

9. After about 15 minutes, flip the cake onto a cake platter and distribute the icing on the cake with a spoon.
10. Slice and serve immediately.

Peanut Butter Banana Bites

Total Prep & Cooking Time: 25 minutes
Makes: 6 Bites
Protein: 24 gm.
Net Carbs: 6 gm.
Fat: 26 gm.
Sugar: 1 gm.
Calories: 192

What you need:

- 1 large banana
- 6 Won Ton Wrappers
- 1/2 cup peanut butter
- coconut oil cooking spray
- 1/8 cup water
- squeeze of lemon

Steps:

1. Prepare a flat sheet covered with baking paper. Set the Won Ton Wrappers side by side.
2. Cut the banana into 6 individual slices and place into a dish. Squeeze the lemon juice over the bananas and place one in the middle of each of the wrappers.
3. Distribute about a teaspoon of peanut butter on top of each of the banana slices.
4. Empty the water into a glass dish.
5. Wet the ends of the wrappers with the water using a pastry brush.
6. Press the opposing corners of the wrapper and then the other two opposing corners to enclose the filling completely.
7. Coat the basket of the air fryer with the cooking spray (olive oil).
8. Arrange the banana bites into the basket and heat at a temperature of 380°F for a total of 6 minutes.
9. Remove to a serving plate and enjoy while hot.

Helpful Tip:
- You can use other fruits such as peaches, apples or berries if you would like to be creative and experiment.
- In addition, different varieties of chocolate chips or raisins can be used in this recipe. Just add a 1/4 cup to the recipe when adding extra ingredients.

Semolina Cake

Total Prep & Cooking Time: 1 hour
Makes: 4 Helpings
Protein: 2 gm.
Net Carbs: 24 gm.
Fat: 6 gm.
Sugar: 5 gm.
Calories: 150

What you need:

- 8 oz. yogurt
- 1/2 olive oil
- 2 1/2 cups semolina flour
- 1/4 tsp. salt
- 8 oz. milk
- 1 1/2 tsp. baking powder
- 8 oz. sugar, granulated
- 1/2 tsp. baking soda
- cooking spray (olive oil)
- 1/2 cup raisins

Steps:

1. Use a food blender to pulse the sugar, olive oil, yogurt, and semolina flour for about 60 seconds until thoroughly blended. Set to the side for about 15 minutes.
2. Heat the air fryer to the temperature of 320°F.
3. Combine the baking soda, raisins, and baking powder until fully incorporated.
4. Coat a pan with the cooking spray (olive oil) and empty the batter into the pan.
5. Smooth with a rubber spatula to make sure it is uniform across the pan.
6. Insert the baking pan into the air fryer basket and steam for approximately 25 minutes.
7. Poke a knife into the center of the cake to ensure it is properly cooked.
8. Remove the pan with oven mitts to a wire rack.
9. Wait about 10 minutes before slicing and serving.

Did you appreciate the wide variety of recipes to try out with your Air Fryer? Leave a review on Amazon to share your views. Thank you!

Index for the Recipes

Garlic Cheese Buns
Hush Puppies
Monkey Bread
Potato Stuffed Bread Rolls
Pull-Apart Rolls
Pumpkin Bread

Chapter 5: Appetizer & Side Recipes

Bacon Brussels Sprouts
Blooming Onion
Bok Choy Salad
Cheesy Ravioli
Chicken Wings
Edamame
Eggplant Parmesan
French Fries
Fried Green Tomatoes
Fried Mushrooms
Fried Okra
Fried Pickles
Grilled Pineapple
Kale Chips
Mozzarella Sticks
Nacho Chips
Onion Rings
Pigs in a Blanket Minis
Potato Chips
Pretzel Poppers
Rib Bites
Roasted Asparagus
Roasted Garlic Potatoes
Spiced Butternut Squash
Sweet Potato Tots
Zucchini Corn Fritters

Chapter 6: Dinner Recipes

Beef and Vegetable Stir Fry
Beef Wellington
Chicken Parmesan
Coconut Shrimp

Crab Cakes
Fried Catfish
Herbed Turkey Breast
Pork Chops
Ribeye Steak
Roast Beef
Rotisserie Chicken
Salmon Fillets
Shrimp Scampi
Tilapia Fillets

Chapter 7: International Recipes

Carne Asada Mexican Taco Plate
Crab Rangoon
Egg Rolls
General Tso's Chicken
Indian Paneer Pappad
Indian Samosas
Mexican Churros
Mexican Corn on the Cob
Spicy Chicken Wontons
Sweet & Sour Tofu and Broccoli
Tempeh Sandwich

Chapter 8: Sweet Treats & Dessert Recipes

Apple Cake
Apple Dumplings
Blackberry Cobbler
Bread and Butter Pudding
Cheesecake Rolls
Chocolate Chip Cookies
Chocolate Lava Cake
Cinnamon Apple Turnovers
Cinnamon Sugar Donuts
Fried Oreos
Fudge Brownies
Fruity Bread Pudding
Lemon Pound Cake
Peanut Butter Banana Bites
Semolina Cake